A FORCE ON THE MOVE

*The Story of the
British Transport Police
1825 - 1995*

A FORCE ON THE MOVE

The Story of the
British Transport Police
1825 - 1995

PAULINE APPLEBY

images PUBLISHING (MALVERN) LTD

First published in Great Britain 1995 by
Images Publishing (Malvern) Ltd.,
The Wells House, Holywell Road, Malvern Wells,
Worcestershire WR14 4LH

British Library Cataloguing in Publication Data

A catalogue record for this book is available
from the British Library

ISBN 1 897817 67 3

Designed and Produced by Images Publishing (Malvern) Ltd.
Printed and Bound in Great Britain by Bookcraft, Bath, Avon.

Contents

To my parents,
Margaret and John Marston,
and Simon, Anne, Clare and Helen.

In the last century the railways transformed the commercial and social landscape of Britain, ushering in a new era of industrial activity and communications. Yet the railways also brought problems: disruption to formerly peaceful towns and villages, new opportunities for crime, and mobility for the criminal. To meet these emerging problems, the transport police were born. Today, the British Transport Police is the national police force for the railways covering England, Scotland and Wales, and the London Underground system. In the forefront of management, organisation and technological development, it truly is *A Force on the Move.*

Desmond O'Brien, OBE, QPM

Chief Constable

To many among the general public, a single badge may appear to differentiate the British Transport Police from their fellow officers in blue. Yet their history is unique and complex – indeed, some might argue that Railway Police existed several years before Robert Peel organised his Metropolitan Force – and a number of major differences make up their constitution. Perhaps the most important of these is that, whilst county police forces are administered by the Home Office, and funded by local and central government, the BTP is the country's only national police force, administered jointly by Government and the railway companies.

Officers of the British Transport Police are easily recognised at the scenes of major disasters or at large national events; however, it is not only then that they are present. They are working everyday to ensure that our rail network is as safe as possible, both pro-actively and re-actively, whilst often dealing with scenes of crime that are moving at 100 miles an hour! As a regular traveller on the railways, I am honoured to have the opportunity to put them in the spotlight.

As an 'outsider' I never imagined that I would be so warmly welcomed by the Force who have supported the project wholeheart-edly from the start. It has been difficult to decide how much of their broad range of work can be included in one book, and the omission of some aspects should not be interpreted as a reflection on their importance. I hope that what follows provides the reader with a good insight into the history and workings of the British Transport Police.

The information has been gleaned from three sources: the British Transport Police Journals (now returned to their rightful place in the Resource Centre at Tadworth); retired and serving members of the Force; and independent research. The Journals provide as superb an insight into the Force at the time of their publication as well as the history of the earliest forces and I am indebted to all of the editors, Leslie James, Willie Neilson, Len Bradley, Bob Butcher, Frank

Radcliffe, Douglas Harrow, Mick Bryan, Bill Phillips and Colin Thomas. Also to Simon Lubin, editor of the Journal's successor, Blue Line, and especially the late William O'Gay QPM, a former Chief Constable of the Force and a prolific and talented writer on police subjects.

At the time of writing, the British Transport Police Historical Society is being formed and I hope that the discussion and debate that the book will no doubt create helps to speed up its establishment. Further details of the Society can be obtained from Sergeant Philip Trendall at Stratford, London, or PC Kevin Gordon at Brighton BTP.

There are many other people without whose help this book would not have been possible. During my research I have had the great pleasure of meeting many officers and civilian staff of the Force, and my thanks go to all of them as well as to the following for their time, encouragement and loan of photographic and other material: Chief Constable Desmond O'Brien, Michael Foster (the inspiration for the book), Les Price, Simon Lubin, Colin Munro, Philip Trendall, Kevin Gordon, Charlie Cook, John Hennigan, Keith Meager and all the staff at Tadworth, Adrian Dwyer, Peter Whent, David Furness, Fred Furness, Martin Taylor, Alistair Napier, Graham Satchwell, Keith Groves, John Leyland, John Lloyd, Betty Glover, Elizabeth Ord, Tom Willoughby, Terry Shelton, Margaret Lyall, Ginge Ablard, Maurice Stamford, Steve Beamon, Brian Deacon, Jim Crowe, Ron Godfrey, David Ayres, Archie MacKenzie, Alan Coupar, Ian McGregor, Dennis Temporal, Andy Douglas, Mick Barry, Damian Thorpe, Viv Head, Randolph Otter, Maggie Reilly, Roger Fergus, Alec Harris, Dick Lyons, Jim Clark, Alan Nalson, Dave Clarke, Polly St Aubyn (Tulliallen), and Reginald Hale, Miss Lorna King, Mr R Tantum, Miss J Ashfield and the Scottish Police College.

Also to David, James, Richard and Jayne who have put up with too much whilst I have been writing this book. Finally to Tony Harold of Images for having faith in the project from the start and I am very much indebted to Catherine Whiting for her exceptional editing skills.

Pauline Appleby,
November 1995

Chapter One

THE RAILWAY POLICE

A NATION IN CHAOS

The late 18th century saw the start of a revolution which was to change the social and economic face of Britain for ever. That revolution was the mechanisation of industry, triggered by a number of catalysts, the most notable of which was the development of steam power. The result was factories, railways and, around them, large industrial towns with new classes of owners and workers.

Traditional cottage industries were better serviced in towns, and coupled with the enclosure of open fields and common land, this meant that farm workers no longer had a way of eking out their meagre wages. Many had no choice but to join the growing exodus to the towns and cities. 'Progress' there too, however, meant that fewer numbers of workers were needed all round. The situation was exacerbated by the defeat of Napoleon at Waterloo in 1815, so ending wars which had begun in 1803, putting thousands of soldiers out of work, along with many of those employed in such periphery industries as ship-building, weapons and uniforms. It was a nation in chaos: falling wages, unemployment, over-crowding, poor health and housing, leading to civil unrest on an unprecedented scale.

In the industrial centres of East Midlands, Lancashire and Yorkshire, the Luddites – a group who saw machinery as the cause of unemployment – took to smashing up the offending contraptions, and further riots and protests followed. The unpopular Tory Government, under its Prime Minister the Duke of Wellington, introduced laws to stop the protests but they were little heeded. On 16th August 1819, some 5,000 cotton workers and their families assembled at St Peter's Field in Manchester. They carried banners that called for 'Liberty and Fraternity' and 'Votes for all', and their meeting, intended to be peaceful, was addressed by Henry Hunt, a Wiltshire farmer famous for his oratory powers. The City Magistrates were of course extremely nervous about the gathering and called in the Yeomanry – volunteer soldiers, mostly businessmen and farmers – to control the crowd and apprehend the speaker. One yeoman, having become separated from the others, panicked and fired his musket into the air. His actions were enough to cause the Magistrates to order a squadron of Hussars into the crowd, slashing their swords around them, creating further panic and mayhem. Within ten minutes, the 'Peterloo Massacre' (a pun on Waterloo) left 11 people dead and over 500 injured. Public outrage was not confined to working men. *The Times,* whose own correspondent was one of those arrested by the Magistrates, led the outcry with an extensive and highly critical report on the affair three days later.

THE BEGINNINGS OF A CIVILIAN POLICE FORCE

Facilities to maintain the peace in this uneasy social background were very limited. Communities – or 'parishes' – were generally governed by their local landowner or landowners, who, in addition to paying occasional neighbourhood watchmen to stand guard over the citizens' property, would annually appoint a 'Constable' (from the Latin, 'keeper of stables', originally a royal appointment). This Constable would swear an oath of allegiance to the Crown and be granted certain powers of arrest; he would be part-time, unpaid and those he apprehended, depending on the scale of their crime, would be brought before the local Magistrate. His duties varied from one area to another – in quiet villages he might be called from his farm just once or twice a year, perhaps to track down a criminal or to search for stolen goods; whilst in larger towns and cities, crime and disorder might be well beyond his powers of control.

In London, 'detective' work was the responsibility of the City Magistrates who, through the initiative of Henry Fielding in the 1750s, employed teams of 'runners' to carry it out from their courts in Bow Street. By 1820 Magistrates had 'Bow Street Runners' working from eight courts, and were beginning to organise London's first uniformed and armed patrols to police the highways and streets on horseback or on foot. It was not enough.

With the crime rate rising daily, and with the disaster of Peterloo at the forefront of people's minds, realisation began to dawn that a proper civilian police force was needed. The responsibility of establishing one fell to newly appointed Home Secretary Sir Robert Peel, who in 1822 began setting up a Force of some 3,000 men to patrol the City of London. Dressed in blue coats, leather belts and white trousers, 'Bobbies' or 'Peelers', as they came to be nicknamed, wore stout top hats, not helmets, and were armed with batons designed to deter enemies of the peace rather than enemies of the nation. However, it took seven years of further persuasion before Parliament passed the Metropolitan Police Act which created a formal force that was to become the model for all city and county forces. In 1835 the Municipal Corporations Act granted counties the power to form their own forces, each headed by a Chief Constable.

THE EARLY RAILWAYS

Robert Peel's Act coincided with major developments in commercial rail services. Until the beginning of the 19th century, all transport in Britain had been by road, river, canal, or by ship around the coast; but the supply of raw materials and goods to and from the growing industries was to generate demand for much greater speed and carrying-capacity than they could cope with. Steam-powered railway engines answered that demand.

Thomas Newcomen was one of the first to develop a steam engine, which he used to pump water out of the mines where he worked; but it was Richard Trevithick, a Cornishman, who designed an engine which applied the power of steam to locomotion. His first successful road locomotive appeared in 1801, and two years later he tried one out on rails. In 1812, at the Middleton railway near Leeds, John Blenkinsop produced a system of steam-powered propulsion that used a combination of track and running rails. Several other designs followed, culminating in 1814 with George Stephenson's locomotive *Blucher* at the Killingworth railway, where Stephenson worked as an engineer. Stephenson was then asked by Edward Pease, a Darlington banker and pioneer of railways, to build one on which coal could be carried to Stockton some 20 miles away. Stephenson agreed, and his own engine *Locomotion* was used to haul the inaugural train on 27th September 1925, at a speed of 15 miles per hour. The Age of the Train had begun.

The ceremonial opening of the Stockton & Darlington Railway.

THE RAILWAY POLICE

The very first railway police were those men employed to watch over the railway and mine workings, to guard against theft and to minimise accidents. The modern five pound note features part of a picture which shows a railway policeman in front of the *Rocket* on Skerne Bridge of the Stockton & Darlington Railway, in 1825.

Policemen were first introduced to maintain order on construction sites like this.

The Stockton & Darlington Act allowed owners of land adjoining the line to build their own branch lines; but this soon proved dangerously impractical, as use of the lines needed to be properly co-ordinated by one body; and so the Stockton & Darlington effectively became the first of a new style of private railway company, to be followed by many others. On 30th June 1826 regulations were incorporated into the Railway's constitution, stating that its 'Police Department' should consist of one Superintendent, four regular officers, and as many gate-keepers as 'circumstance required'. The Superintendent would earn 20/- a week and was to be provided with a great coat, two dress coats, two pairs of trousers and two hats every year. Officers would receive 18/- per week and would be provided with a great coat every two years, and one dress coat, two pairs of trousers and one hat each year.

The regulations further stated:

> 'All policemen and other servants of the company are required in the first place and before every other consideration to consult the personal safety of the passengers and all others on or about the Railway; in order to do this, the strictest attention to the regulations is enjoined upon them. Except in the cases where the observations might be attended with risk, in such instances they must immediately report such deviation and the cause of it in the proper quarter. [The duty of the Superintendent was to] exercise a general care over all parts of the company and property and enforce the instructions of the company without regard to hours, independent of any other party except the Directors and Secretary and that the Officers and Gatekeeper be placed under his especial care and direction . . . [It continues] that the Superintendent and 1 Officer do reside at Darlington and 1 Officer at Shildon, 1 at Stockton and 1 at Middlesborough. That the Superintendent and 1 of the Officers in rotation do attend weekly meetings of the Board of Directors when the Superintendent shall produce a condensed report of all the proceedings of the Police during the last week. Hours of work – Officers; 6 am to 8 pm, with a suitable allowance of time for meals and each man do attend 4 hrs on line every Sunday. That they do perform any extra duty promptly, leaving the remuneration to the Board, that they perform night duty whenever and where the Superintendent shall direct. That they carefully watch the speed of the engines and invariably report any enginemen stopping at public houses.'

There is further mention of the Stockton & Darlington police force in a letter of 1839, in which the Company Directors request details of fatal accidents on the railway, and refer to the 'Police Reports' made to the committee since its start in 1825.

One of the earliest illustrations of a railway policeman can be found on Wallis's 'Locomotive Game of Road Adventures', based on the adventures that travellers might encounter on an early railway journey. It consists of a folded linen sheet covered by 49 hand-coloured aquatint pictures.
Photo: NRM/Science & Society Picture Library

The Liverpool & Manchester Railway was the next great landmark – the first to carry both goods and passengers and to join two major cities. Like the Stockton & Darlington, the Company employed a police force at the construction stages, records suggest as early as 1827.

The line was officially opened to the public on 15th September 1830, attracting great crowds, among them such dignitaries as the Prime Minister the Duke of Wellington. His presence, coupled with the public's bad feeling towards him, meant that every section of track had to be closely guarded. A witness described the scene:

> 'The local garrison was under arms and at various points within the site of the railway, cavalry were placed. Without this display of military force there would certainly have been a breach of the peace, the populous having taken possession of many parts of the Railway.'

In addition to crowd control problems, the ceremony was marred by the death of the Right Honourable William Huskisson, the Liverpool MP and President of the Board of Trade. Huskisson disobeyed Company orders by leaving his post on the *Northumbrian*; he was crushed between that engine and the *Rocket*, hauling a train on the adjacent track. Stephenson rushed him by train to hospital in Eccles, where he died later that night. Ironically, Huskisson's last journey was the fastest train journey in history so far, reaching speeds of up to 36 miles per hour. His death highlighted the dangers posed by railways, and a need for a separate force to police them.

Some 60 officers were soon employed under the supervision of Liverpool & Manchester Chief of Police Captain Brook. They were posted at watch huts or 'station houses', forerunners of passenger stations and goods depots, at one mile intervals along the line from where they could maintain 'a continual line of communication'. Their duties were to guard the railroad, prevent or give notice of obstructions, lend assistance in the case of accidents and oversee procedures at the station houses. Rules and regulations specified:

> 'Every gate-man or policeman shall light his gate or station-lamp at dusk, and shall have his hand-lamp constantly trimmed and burning, and ready to give signals as required . . . during a fog or thick weather – whenever a coach-train stops at any of the stations or places for taking up or setting down passengers the gateman or policeman shall immediately run 400 yards behind the train, or so far as may be necessary to warn any coming engine, in order to prevent it running against the other.'

A railway policeman signalling to a night train, 1844.

Operating a station post signal, 1844.

For performing these duties satisfactorily, officers were paid 17/6d per week, a sum which was increased to 21/- in 1831. In March of the following year, the number of policemen was reduced to 32, but by 1842 it had risen again to 59, with officers placed under the supervision of station engineers. Their uniform consisted of a blue frock coat and top hat, with the later addition of a great coat.

THE SPECIAL CONSTABLES ACT OF 1831

Prior to 1831, the appointment of police officers was a private affair carried out by the railway company, but as the potential of railways was realised, Parliament felt compelled to intercede. The Special Constables Act was the first Parliamentary Act to enable railway companies to officially appoint 'Special Constables' to preserve order on the construction sites of the railway, to patrol and protect the line and to control the movement of traffic. Sworn in by local magistrates under a statute originally passed in 1673, Constables were financed by local authorities, and their jurisdiction was confined to that of the Justices who had appointed them. However, with lines running from one jurisdiction into another, this soon gave rise to conflict, so Parliament began extending jurisdiction along the whole of the line. It was an important development in the nature of police jurisdiction, although as yet rather limiting, for officers had no powers of arrest *outside* railway property and criminals have a habit of running away from the scene of their crime!

Under an Act of 1833 the London & Birmingham Railway Company became the first to obtain statutory power to appoint Special Constables in this way. It read:

'That it shall be lawful for two or more Justices of the Peace of any of the said Counties of Middlesex, Hertford, Buckingham, Northampton, Warwick and Worcester, or for the liberty of Saint Alban, or the City of Coventry, from time to time to appoint such persons as shall be nominated to them by any three of the Directors of the said Company for that purpose, to be Special Constables within the said Railway and other works and every or any part thereof; and every person so appointed shall take an Oath, to be administered by any of the Justices of the Peace for any of the said Counties or places, duly to execute the Office of a Constable for the said premises; and every person so appointed and sworn as aforesaid shall have the power to act as a Constable for the preservation of the peace, and for the Security of Persons and Property, against felonies and other unlawful acts, within the limits of the said premises, and shall have, use, exercise and enjoy all such powers, Authorities, protections and privileges for the apprehending of offenders, as well by night as by day, and for doing all acts, matters and things for the prevention, discovery and prosecution of felonies and other offences, and for the preservation of peace as Constables duly appointed now have by the laws and statutes of this kingdom; and it shall be lawful for the said justices, or any three or more Directors of the said Company, to dismiss or remove any such Constable from his office of Constable; and upon every such dismissal or removal all powers, authorities, protection and privileges, by virtue of such appointment as aforesaid, vested in any person so dismissed or removed, shall wholly cease.'

Inspector Bedford of the Metropolitan Police was appointed Superintendent of the London & Birmingham and, by 1839, was in charge of ten Inspectors and 90 Constables. In addition to being sworn in by the Railway Company, London & Birmingham men were sworn in as County Constables, which meant their jurisdiction extended into the towns. As with the Liverpool & Manchester, officers were stationed at intervals of a mile to a mile and a half along the line, and were on duty from 30 minutes before the first train of the day, to 30 minutes after the last train. Their uniform was modelled on that of the Metropolitan Police, but with a green rather than blue coat. Pay was also on par with the Metropolitan, until 1842 when Inspectors had their salary reduced from 30/- to 25/- per week.

As railways and the men who policed them became part of the establishment, full-time Constables lost the prefix 'Special'; although in the course of the next century, a number of special circumstances would arise when part-time, unpaid 'Special' Constables would be appointed.

THE NAVVIES

With crime developing at a similar pace to the railway network itself, and the railways themselves providing criminals with an extremely quick and effective means of escape, the early Railway Policeman's lot the majority of his time – he had to deal with theft of goods, damage to installations, crimes against the public, the public themselves; and, in the beginning, the very men drafted in to build the railways.

The Navigators, or 'Navvies' as they came to be known, were a huge force of some 500,000 men, comprising ex-farm workers, canal builders and soldiers returning from the Napoleonic Wars. Labouring under highly dangerous conditions, and using only shovels and wheelbarrows, each man could dig a trench 35 metres long, a metre wide and a metre deep in a day. It is certain that without them the Industrial Revolution would never have developed at the speed it did; but their reputation was as appalling as the conditions in which they worked. One contemporary account described them as

> ' . . . possessed of all the daring recklessness of the smuggler without any of his redeeming qualities, their ferocious behaviour can be equalled only by the brutality of their language. From being long known to each other they in general act in concert and put at defiance any local constabulary force.'

Police officers were hard pressed to control them; the Church almost completely despaired of them; and they struck terror into the heart of the populous. In 1836 the inhabitants of Slough begged for some officers of the Metropolitan Police to be sent to protect them from the men building the railway as 'the parochial constables were totally unable to afford sufficient protection'. Under pressure to do something, two years later the Government passed an Act of Parliament granting rural authorities the power to recruit Special Constables, but to charge the cost of them to the Railway Companies. It was intended that this would provide policing across a larger area of the country; however, their action led to bitter complaints by rate payers, who believed their police were being used to protect private property, that is, the railways. So, on 10th August 1838, a further Act was passed which required Railway Companies to provide their own police. The Act talked of how

'. . . Great mischiefs have arisen by the outrageous and
unlawful behaviour of labourers and others employed on the
railroads, canals and other public works by reason whereof the
appointment of Special Constables is often necessary for keeping the peace and for the protection of inhabitants and
security of property in the neighbourhood of such public
works whereby great expenses have been cast upon the public
rates of counties and other districts chargeable with such
expenses.'

But the Navvies were never far from trouble and over the years when
the railways were being built, there were numerous incidents. One of
the most notable took place in 1846 when two Navvies from the North
British Railway were arrested for stealing watches and placed in a
lock-up. Their colleagues marched to the Police House to protest and
murdering the local constable. The same year saw Navvies tunnel
under the floor of a lock-up in Swindon to release one of their friends.
Three years later saw the 'Battle of Mickleton' on the North British
Railway, when two Navvy armies, one of them led by Isambard
Kingdom Brunel himself, marched towards each other to resolve a
contractual dispute using sticks and cudgels! One ganger was
murdered and the Riot Act had to be read out twice before order was
restored. The perpetrators of the murder were subsequently hanged on
a makeshift scaffold beside the track.

In 1851 John Francis, in his *History of the English Railway*,
characterised the feelings of many concerning the Navvies:

'The dread of such men as these spread throughout a rural
community is striking. They injured everything they
approached, from their huts to the parts of the railway they
were working on, over corn and grass they tore down
embankments, injured young plantations, made gaps in
hedges with no regard to damage of the property invaded.
Game disappeared from the most sacred preserves; game
keepers were defied, and the country gentlemen, who had

imprisoned country rustics by the dozen for violating the law, shrank in despair at the Railway Navigator. They defied the law; broke open prisons; released their comrades and slew policemen.'

In opposition to this popular view, Samuel Peto MP, one of Britain's two biggest railway contractors, spoke in Parliament that same year:

'I know from personal experience that if you pay [the Navvy] well, and show you care for him, he is the most faithful and hard working creature in existence; but if you find him working for fourpence a day, and that paid in potatoes and meal, can we wonder that the results are as we find them. But give him . . . remuneration for his services, show you appreciate those services, and you may be sure you put an end to all agitation. He will be your faithful servant.'

THE ROLE OF THE RAILWAY POLICE

When the Great Western Railway police force was formed in 1835 it consisted of one Inspector, four sub-Inspectors, and 33 Constables who, working in 12 hour shifts, covered the 24.5 miles of the Paddington to Maidenhead stretch. Within a few years the original force of 38 men had grown to over 170, and the creator of the GWR – Isambard Kingdom Brunel – was able to report to a Parliamentary Select Committee that they were meeting the average of 1.5 policemen per mile along the London to Bristol line, including those on stations. Inspectors were appointed to take charge of the London and Bristol Divisions and the railway's growth resulted in the formation of a third, Northern Division. Constables were considered to be the most important class of railwayman and had all such powers 'as Constables duly appointed now have by the laws and statutes of this Kingdom'.

The uniform of the early GWR Police was also modelled on that of the Metropolitan Force. It comprised a dresscoat, top hat and boots, with officers sporting the letters 'GWR' and their number on a stand up collar in scarlet cloth, and Inspectors a one and a quarter inch red stripe down the trouser leg. The top hat gave way to a more comfortable – and less expensive – cap in 1859. Each Constable was also issued with a wooden truncheon, 18 inches long and elaborately decorated with a crown and the letters 'GWR' in gold paint; whilst the Inspector's staff comprised a short hollow brass and ebony tube with a removable cap in the shape of a crown, in which their warrant card was carried. Watches – a rare item amongst working men of the time – were also issued so that Constables could ensure a suitable time delay between trains entering each section of track, thus avoiding collision. It is thought that this is the origin of the saying 'If you want to know the time, ask a policeman'.

Great Western Railway.

POLICE DEPARTMENT.

Detail of Constable's Duty from Wednesday, the   day of   to Wednesday, the   day of   ,   186

Collar No.   Name   Rank

Beat

To come on Duty at   o'Clock.

To go off Duty at   o'Clock.

Dinner Hour from   o'Clock to   o'Clock.

Every man is required to Report himself to his Superior, on coming on and leaving Duty, and he must on no pretence whatever leave his Beat at any other time than that specified above.

Constable's Signature

Sub-Inspector's Signature

The Constable's Warrant Card.

The Inspector's staff.

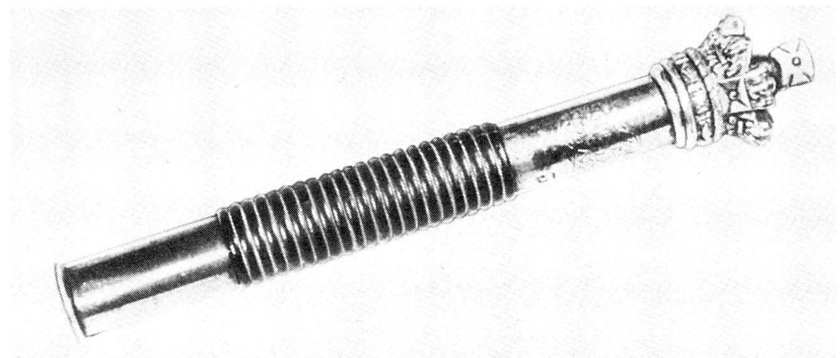

Policemen controlled the railway traffic by means of hand signals from wooden sentry boxes. These boxes were just large enough for one man to stand up in, and were furnished with a seat but no door. Positioned on a pivot, they allowed the man to turn the box in order to protect himself from the elements. By 1838 they were also equipped with lamps to facilitate night-signals. The 'best' officers were chosen to operate the switches on the line and were referred to as 'Switchmen'; they received a higher rate of pay than the ordinary Constable, as well as an annual bonus.

Illustrated articles were frequently published in magazines and journals, such was the public interest in the new railway phenomenon.

A policeman's lamp. The lenses were white (all clear); green (caution); and red (stop).

Constable Coghlan, who walked the entire line from Birmingham to London, described his duties in *The Iron Road Book*, (published 1838):

> 'The Officer was provided with a red and green flag for use during the day and a lamp with a red, green and white shutter for night. When the engine driver in charge of the train was approaching during darkness, if a white light was shown the train carried on at that speed. A green light caused it to slacken speed and a red light was for it to stop. During the day, flags were used for the same purpose.'

The Great Western Railway regulations of 1841 described its police duties thus:

> '. . . generally to consist in the preservation of order in all the stations and on the line of railway. They are to give and

receive signals; to keep the line free from casual or wilful obstructions; to assist in case of accidents; to caution strangers of danger on the railway; to remove intruders of all descriptions; to superintend and manage the crosses or switches; to give notice of arrivals and departures; to direct persons to the entrance to the stations or sheds; to watch movements of embankments or cuttings; to inspect the rails and solidity of timber; to guard and watch the company's premises; and to convey the earliest information on every subject to their appointed station or superior officer.'

The London & North Western Railway rule book of 1849 stated that Inspectors should patrol their district daily, checking that officers, pointsmen and gatemen were at their posts clean, sober, attentive and conversant with their orders; that the points were in good working order, clean and oiled; and that each police box had a copy of the standing orders relating to police signals and duties. Any irregularities had to be reported to the Superintendent.

Following the opening of the Liverpool & Manchester Railway, officers were also expected to assist with the growing passenger 'station duties'. For example, passengers had to apply to a Constable if they wished to purchase a ticket; he required 24 hours notice and 'noted name, address, place of birth, age, occupation [and] reason for journey in his book.' Only if the journey was considered to be for a 'just and loyal cause' would a ticket be issued!

A Constable's normal working day was 12 hours, six days a week; and pay varied between 10 shillings and 23 shillings a week depending on the size of the railway. Falling asleep on duty was a dismissable offence and drunkenness while 'conducting traffic' was an offence liable to prosecution.

Portrait in oils of Constable Metcalfe of the Stockton & Darlington Railway.

THE ROYAL COMMISSION REPORT OF 1839

In time, switching from traffic control to police work to station work and vice versa was to prove very unsatisfactory, as illustrated by the case of one unfortunate officer from Ilford who was blamed for a train collision because he was dealing with a disturbance involving trespassers when he should have been changing some points!

When a Royal Commission was set up in 1836 to decide on the best means of establishing an efficient Constabulary Force in England and Wales, it naturally touched upon the subject of the Railway Police. The Commission's panel of advisors, included one of the first

Metropolitan Commissioners, Colonel Rowan; Mr Charles Lefevere and Mr Edwin Chadwick, a social reformer. In their report of 1839 they noted that the Railroad Companies had recently been compelled to maintain a police force and begged

> ' . . . leave to submit an objection to that measure as precedent. If it were adopted as a general principle that voluntary associations should protect themselves and for that purpose should through their agents be invested with the power and protection belonging to Officers hitherto appointed for the protection of the public at large, each description of property and each description of personal interests would have its own peculiar police forces . . .'

They made note of the fact that there had already been a number of complaints that Railway Police protected the companies against passengers without protecting the passengers themselves, and that they had been known to suppress and conceal information about accidents. Mr Andrew MacManus, the Chief Constable of Hull, suggested to the Commission that 'property policemen' should be appointed at the railway stations whose business it would be to 'observe suspicious characters'. Mr MacManus was generally critical of the Railway Police, whom, he said, he had seen wearing the same uniform as the Metropolitan Police, and perceived amongst the Constables 'much familiarity and incivility'. He suggested that the police should be under one control and with a proper system of communication, in order to provide better services, with less men at less expense.

Although some of this criticism was justified, it gave no credit to what Railway Policemen *were* doing, nor to the fact that maintaining order on the railways was sometimes beyond their capacity. That year, for example, fighting had broken out between English and Irish Navvies employed on the construction of the Chester & Birkenhead Railway, and it had been four days before order was restored – and only then because of the intervention of a detachment of infantry.

Railways were not popular with everyone. Landowners feared the countryside would be ruined by them. This cartoon of 1847 depicts 'Railway Policeman Subthorpe' – a politician hostile to railways – arresting a train. The caption reads:
*   'Come, it's high time you were taken to the House; you've done quite enough mischief.'*

THE JOHN TAWELL ARREST

The Railway Policeman's ability to deal with crime improved as lineside duties were reduced. With the introduction in the early 1840s of mechanical signalling and the electric telegraph, which could send messages much faster than he could, the policeman was freed from the time-consuming business of regulating traffic. No longer did he have to run a mile or more to warn a train of an obstruction on the track! These developments are well illustrated by the circumstances surrounding the arrest of John Tawell on 1st January 1845. Tawell had been convicted for forgery and sentenced to 21 years transportation to Australia, but after just seven years he had managed to return to

England, where he married a rich widow and for a while lived a very comfortable life with servants attending to his every need. Tawell had also had an association with one Sara Hart of Salt Hill, near Slough; and believing he had told her too much about his sordid past, he decided to murder her. He achieved this by poisoning her glass of stout, but her last deathly shriek was loud enough to alert her neighbours, among them the Reverend E Champnes, Vicar of Upton-Cum-Chavley. From a description by a witness who had seen Tawell leaving Sara's cottage, Reverend Champnes was able to follow him to the station at Slough, where he spotted him dressed as a Quaker, and boarding the first class compartment of a train headed for Paddington. Champnes informed the station master who sent the now historic message from Telegraph Cottage, just outside the station, to Paddington:

> 'A murder has just been committed at Salt Hill and the suspected murderer was seen to take a first-class ticket for London by the train which left Slough at 7.42 pm. He is in the garb of a Kwaker [the telegraph code did not include the letter Q] with a brown great coat on which reaches down to his feet. He is in the last compartment of the second first-class carriage.'

A short while later the clerk at Paddington sent the following reply:

> 'The up train has arrived and a person answering in every respect the description given by telegraph came out of the compartment mentioned. The man got into a New-road omnibus and Sergeant Williams into the same.'

Sergeant William Williams of the Great Western Railway Police had donned a plain coat over his police uniform and followed Tawell to several coffee houses, and finally to a lodging house in Scott's Yard, Cannon Street, where he reported Tawell's whereabouts to the

Metropolitan Police. The following morning Williams and Inspector Wiggins of D Division of the Metropolitan Police together arrested Tawell as the Jerusalem Coffee House. It was Inspector Wiggins who actually took Tawell into custody because, as Sergeant Williams said in his evidence during the trial, 'I am no officer off the station.' Tawell was tried at Aylesbury Assizes and sentenced to death. He was executed on 28th March 1845 at Aylesbury.

Telegraph Cottage at Slough Station.

There have been many such dramatic moments in the history of the Railway Police. One of the most bizarre occurred in the early 1850s. In 1851 a train running between Brighton and Lewes struck an obstruction and the driver and one passenger were killed. A youth suspected of causing the obstruction was arrested and interviewed but, as there was no evidence, he was released. Exactly one year later, to the day, at the very same spot, the youth was struck by lightning and killed.

THE HEYDAY OF THE RAILWAYS

Railways were always seen as an improvement on the road system, and in the mid-19th century, nothing could stop their expansion across the country. In 1854 the North Eastern Railway was born out of a merger between the York, Newcastle & Berwick Railway, the York & North Midland Railway and the Leeds Northern Railway. These companies were themselves the result of earlier amalgamations involving over 20 companies, including the famous Stockton & Darlington Railway. On its inception, the North Eastern Railway had a capital expenditure of £20 million, operated 700 route miles and owned 44 acres of dockland. By 1865 its mileage had grown to 1,200 and the company had become renowned for its quality of staff and the training they received.

PC Runnicles of the South Wales Railway, c. 1860

By this time 51,000 miles of track had been laid nationally, and 3,000 stations built so that almost all were within reasonable reach of the population. An Act in 1844 had ruled that all railways must run one train a day which stopped at every station and charged only 1d a mile. Known as 'Parliamentary trains', they enabled ordinary working people to undertake long journeys – and journey they most certainly did. Seaside resorts, previously the domain of the wealthy, who arrived by stage coach, soon became immensely popular with working classes. Piers and promenades were built, and boarding house sprang up to entertain and accommodate them; whilst wealthier holiday-makers stayed at hotels with names like the Grand. Travelling by train was by no means comfortable, but it was exciting. For the first time in history, the whole population was becoming truly mobile.

There were three classes of railway carriage. First class, which only the wealthy could afford, resembled the old stage coach; although with six seats and elbow rests, it had considerably more room. The London & Birmingham Railway also introduced a special coach for Post Office traffic with first-class accommodation inside and the mail carried in boxes on the roof. Second class passengers, who had previously travelled on the stage coach roofs, were provided with very basic carriages, but they were still better than being exposed to the elements. Those companies which offered third class travel provided open wagons with benches and holes drilled in the floor to prevent puddles forming in wet weather – contravening the 1844 Railway Act which ruled that trucks on Parliamentary trains must be covered. One contemporary source talked of the 'Teaming hundreds' who travelled in these wagons:

> ' . . . rough sailors with tarry hands and bronzed faces, pretty servant maids, Jewish peddlers, Irish labourers, soldiers of furlough, housewives and farmwives, taciturn clerks and merry tipplers, excited children and worried mothers.'

'Teeming hundreds'
travelled on the
railways.

During the 1870s, second class was abolished and an improved third class became the norm. By the 1880s, lighting, heating and lavatories were standard.

It wasn't only holiday makers who used the railways. Middle classes began moving to suburbs around the overcrowded towns and cities, from which they could commute by train. Around major junctions, railway towns developed. Crewe, for example, was originally just a farmhouse but it became a major link for railways of the Midlands, North West England and Scotland; and it was the Railway Company's responsibility to police it – indeed, the company combined with the local magistrates to build the town's first police station. However, with their duties extending to cover a town's needs rather than just the railway's, officers found they were taking on the role of bailiffs – seizing goods for non-payment of rent.

London, Brighton & South Coast Railwaymen. From left to right: Ticket Collector, Ticket Inspector, Station Superintendent, Station Inspector, Guard and Policeman.

Following the County Police Act of 1856, it was no longer necessary to patrol the entire length of track, and Railway Constables were withdrawn to the larger stations and junctions. The growing complexity of the signalling apparatus also brought about a special grade of 'railway signalman', although police officers continued to operate switches for some years to come.

[opposite]
A letter of 1858 referring to the appointment of Special Constables.

Chief Constables Office
Carlisle
21/9/1858

To: John Wakefield Esq
Chairman of the South Durham and Lancashire
Union Railway, Kendal

Dear Sir

Referring to my verbal reports to yourself and Mr Thompson on the subject of some additional Special Constables for the purpose of preserving order along your new line of railway called the South Durham and Lancashire Union Railway I have the honour to inform you that I have recently received several complaints from the inhabitants of Ravenstoudale and other districts through which the line runs, to the effect that serious disturbances have occurred in consequence of the large number of persons employed on the line and complaining that life and property is not properly protected, I regret very much that the limited constabulary force of the county is not sufficient to afford the protection required. I therefore feel it my duty to apply to the Railway Company to authorize appointment of two or three constables for the purpose.

I may mention that the magistrates have power to appoint a sufficient number of constables for this duty under the powers of the Act 5th or 6th Win 4 Calp. 43 Section 1 and afterwards to charge the expenses connected herewith to the railway company under the powers of the Act 1st and 2nd bid; Caps 80, Sections 1 and 3.

I trust however that the necessity of making an application upon the subject to the magistrates will be obviated by the company granting the requisite protection.

I have the honour to be your most humble servant.

[Signed]
Chief Constable for the Counties of Cumberland and Westmoreland.

In 1859 Superintendent Collard of the Great Western Railway retired as Chief of Police. As was the case with other Railway Police forces, uniformed Constables, known as 'traffic police', came to lack central organisation; instead they were employed by the passenger and goods departments and came under the control of the individual station masters or goods agents. This gave rise to some controversy; for example, those employed in the goods department of Paddington Station complained that they were receiving less pay than those in the passenger department who were able to supplement their incomes with tips from passengers whose luggage they carried!

Candidates to join the Force had to apply to the divisional traffic Superintendent, and, on appointment, be under 30 years of age, five feet ten inches in height, and with a chest measurement of not less than 34 inches. Pay on the Great Western Railway commenced at 21 shillings per week – the same rate as the North Eastern Railway; whilst the Great Northern Railway offered 23 and the London & South Western only 19.

In time, the Railway Police gradually began to assert their authority, not just with the public, but with the railway companies, too, and on a variety of matters. In 1877 one policeman named Vallentine Salvage, together with 18 other policemen and hundreds of railwaymen of the South Eastern Railway, decided to protest about the Company's prohibition of staff moustaches. Unhappy about their bare faces,   they all signed a petition and sent it to their General Manager. It   read:

'We, the undersigned, being inspectors, guards, ticket collectors and other employees in the service of South Eastern Railway having been heretofore prohibited from wearing moustachios by the regulations of the Company's service and believing and being advised that the wearing of the moustachios is a protection against the inclemency of the weather and for divers other reasons beg most respectfully to solicitate your aid in abrogating or obtaining the abrogation of the aforesaid prohibitory rule, by your doing which you will confer on us a great benefit for which we shall be most grateful.'

Officers also began to have their jurisdiction extended. Section 38 of the London & North Western Railway Act of 1868 gave powers for Special Constables to act up to 300 yards away from the railway, although when outside railway premises they were subject to rules and regulations laid down by the local 'watch' committee. However, only six Special Constables could be appointed in any city, town or borough, and in consequence the majority were almost powerless. It was not until 1912 that the LNWR Act (Section 47) abolished limitations on the number of officers sworn in, at the same time

An accident at Norton Fitzwarren. A policeman guards the wreckage from sightseers and souvenir hunters.

empowering officers to follow and arrest persons who had committed offences on the railway property away from the railway's premises.

In 1877 six Constables of the Great Western were also granted jurisdiction up to half a mile from the railway, with the further provision that they were liable to a 40 shilling penalty if they failed to show their warrant cards on request. In 1899 Special Constables of the Great Western Railway were granted powers to follow and arrest, and in 1912, in line with the London & North Western, the limitation on numbers was lifted.

Railway staff, including a Constable, of the London, Brighton & South Coast Railway at Clapham Junction, c. 1900.

CAPTAIN HORWOOD OF THE NORTH EASTERN RAILWAY POLICE

By 1909 the North Eastern Railway Police Force comprised some 200 officers divided into two areas, North and South. Competition between the two was fierce. The North was headed by Superintendent Darrell, based at Newcastle, and the South by Superintendent Dobbie based at York. Superintendent Darrell was referred to as a 'terror' and it was not unknown for officers to faint before him at disciplinary hearings. These railway policemen received 23/- per week for 10 hours work a day, seven days a week, with one rest day a month (although in practice this day was often worked). They retired at 70 years of age, some having taken advantage of the Stockton & Darlington superannuation fund that allowed them to retire on two-thirds wages.

The uniform was a peaked cap, a frocked tail coat with two rows of brass buttons, and thick melton cloth trousers. Duties included

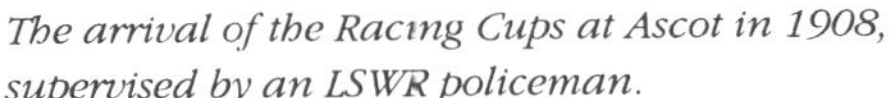

The arrival of the Racing Cups at Ascot in 1908, supervised by an LSWR policeman.

maintaining law and order, ringing a large hand bell to call passengers to trains and replacing guards or ticket collectors if they failed to report for duty. Constables were also required to carry passengers' luggage. Race meetings and football matches demanded additional policing, and officers were expected to call out train times to the waiting travellers.

In 1910, on the retirement of the two Superintendents, Captain Horwood, an officer with the 5th Royal Irish Lancers, was appointed Chief of Police. After making contact with every officer and seeking his opinion, Horwood single-handedly reorganised the Force by creating a system of ranks, modernising the uniform and re-assigning duties so that menial tasks were removed from the list of responsibilities. Horwood also oversaw a dramatic improvement in working conditions, as a result of which officers worked a nine hour day, six days a week. The maximum wage for a Constable was 34/- per week with 1/6d per week boot allowance, three months full and three months half sick pay and 12 free railway tickets per year. Divisions were established at Newcastle, Darlington and York (although Darlington was later eliminated).

1912 saw the introduction of the North Eastern Railway's own Superannuation Scheme. Within just two years these changes had been effected, and the Force gained a reputation second to none. Many officers from civil and other Forces applied for transfer to NER, much to the consternation of the other Chief Constables who requested Horwood not to accept them.

[opposite top right] NER Police Inspector in his jacket suit.

[left] Summer uniform for PCs and Sergeants.

[bottom left] Winter uniform of NER Constables and Sergeants.

[bottom right] NER Police Overcoat.

Peter Park was a policeman during those days of great change and in the British Transport Journal of July 1957 recalled the famous Dickman case.

> 'It was the sixth train murder in Britain, the first being in 1864. A colliery cashier named John Innes Nisbet was murdered in a train between Newcastle and Alnmouth and robbed of the wages cash. The train was the 10.27 am from Newcastle and Nisbet's body with five bullet wounds was found in a compartment by a porter. I well remember the hearing at the police court. The defence was that Dickman, who had been arrested, was not the murderer and that a mistake had been made in identification. The evidence against him was entirely circumstantial. The defence nearly succeeded but Dickman was committed for trial and subsequently convicted and hanged.'

Park also recalled how hard they sometimes had to be:

> 'When we took the women [prostitutes] off the boats at West Hartlepool we used a push-cart to take them to the police station. We used to strap their ankles to the handles and hold them down on the cart.'

Being a reservist, Horwood was called back to the colours in the Great War where he was appointed Provost Marshal, taking with him several other NER men who had been specially enlisted to help him. After the War he initiated the most comprehensive training programme outside the Metropolitan Police, following which he was appointed Commissioner of the said Force. Mr E Barrell, Horwood's Chief Clerk, replaced him as Chief of Police in 1914.

Frederick James Adams 1869– 1937. Mr Adams served on the South East Chatham Railway and Midland Railway.
Courtesy of Mr R. E. Tantum

SCOTTISH RAILWAYS

During the heyday of railway travel over 200 steam railways were created in Scotland alone. Two of particular note, both incorporated in 1845, were the North British Railway, running from Berwick to Edinburgh, and the Caledonian Railway, running from Carlisle to Glasgow, Edinburgh, and Perth, with its first service to London in 1848. Many lesser railways merged to form bigger holdings. 'The Caley', as the Caledonian became known, was among them, growing and prospering as it absorbed the Scottish North Eastern, the Scottish Midland Junction, and a number of local lines including Garkirk,

Coatbridge, the Wishaw & Coltness, the Clydebank Junction, the Pollock & Govan and the Glasgow & Greenock lines. Many of these lines would have employed some sort of police presence. The minutes of a meeting of the Directors of the Banff, Portsoy & Strathisla Railway Company in 1858 record the approval of the appointment of two constables under an application to the Sheriff and the Company who authorised them: James McKenzie and John Grant, at £1.18/-89 and £1.17/-4 respectively, for 'their attendance and outlays on pay days'. On 21st January the following year, the Company Secretary was instructed to arrange 'so as the company's two constables should be at the different places of payment on pay days, and if possible to make the payment at the Banff end on different days from the payments at Portsoy and Cornhill so as to allow the constables to be at Banff on the days of pay there.'

Opening of the Great North of Scotland Railway, 30th September, 1854. A Railway Policeman gives the all-clear signal.

*Officer of the
North British Railway.*

The Highland Railways are also known to have had their own police force – as in England, a necessary deterrent to over-boisterous behaviour on the part of the Navvies. In *Short Holidays in Open Boats*, W H McPherson describes an encounter with the Mallaig Railway Navvies in June of 1898:

'There were police block-houses every two miles along the line of the railway and some pretty lively scenes were enacted during our stay. But it was wonderful to see the tact and skill with which the police managed them. One sergeant, with his cane, in the midst of a half drunken mob of navvies, threatening him with extermination was a fearsome sight! But one came to see by degrees that they had in reality great respect for him, and more or less recognised the fact of his authority.'

Inverness had no police force of its own; instead, a constable from the Burgh Police was permanently seconded to the railway station and it is thought that this may have been a common situation with many of the smaller companies.

Edinburgh & Glasgow Railway notice, 1863.

Staff of the Caledonian Railway.

Prior to 1923, the Caledonian and the North British were the only Scottish Railways known to have had official police departments. Each branch of the Caledonian handled its own police matters, with staff sworn in under Section 60 of the Caledonian Railway (General Powers) Act of 1899. Among the various grades of railwaymen promoted to these posts, was Alexander Lang, a bookmaker at Mossend. He moved up to the position of ticket collector, Assistant Detective in Glasgow, and eventually the first and only Chief of Police of the Caledonian Railway. The 25th December 1916 issue of the *Daily Record* and *Mail* explains his appointment:

'The Detective and Police work of the railways has been growing in importance, and hitherto each department has dealt with its own particular cases. The directors of the

Caledonian company have decided upon a new departure, and from January 1st, the police and detectives of the various departments will be amalgamated. Mr A Lang has been selected to take charge of the new Police department, which will cover the whole of the Caledonian System from Aberdeen to Carlisle. His headquarters will be in Glasgow and he will be known as the Chief of Police.'

Mr Lang was not adverse to publicity and wrote a regular column for the *Glasgow Weekly Herald* entitled 'Crime on the Line – Railway Mysteries that I have solved.' During a talk to an esteemed audience, he spoke of the specific need for Railway Police forces.

' . . . the Railway Companies although being the largest ratepayers in the county, can only claim from the civil police the same protection for their property and the property of traders, temporarily in their possession, as is afforded to the humblest ratepayer and his possessions. You will appreciate that such protection is far from sufficient for railway property with its ramifications extending into every corner of the country and in many instances goods etc have – of necessity – to lie in open yards and sidings with no protection whatever and with such opportunity presenting itself, the thief was quick to take advantage resulting in the railway companies being called upon to pay claims amounting to many thousands of pounds and to meet this situation the establishment of special police forces for the railways became necessary. The Government is very jealous of the police forces of the country and (before establishing a police force) you must first show cause for the necessity of the establishment of a special police force, then you must introduce a Bill in parliament requesting authority and if the Bill is passed and becomes an Act then you may proceed with the establishment of the police force.'

Lang quoted figures for railway crimes during 1917 and 1922: no fewer than 2,606 persons were arrested and convicted for theft from the company's premises and 1,057 persons were arrested for attempting to defraud the company.

Chief Inspector Alexander Lang

He also offered an interesting description of Railway Police officers:

'To the ordinary person who does not come much in contact with the police or the individual who does not take any interest whatever in such, the constable appears a rather dull, drab sort of person who moves about with slow measured step and appears to take little or no interest or notice of things about him, but I have no doubt it will surprise many to know that that is part of his training, for it is obvious that if an officer makes himself unnecessarily conspicuous, his chances of making headway are remote. While an officer is moving about in the manner referred to he is at the same time taking mental note of every little detail, which in very many instances becomes of much value to him.'

This reproduced newspaper page carries the following article text:

III.—" BEWARE OF CARDSHARPERS!"

ON reading the newspaper report of a prosecution for cardsharping in a railway train one is apt to ask why such pests are permitted to travel by rail. This question is perhaps best answered by asking another—"How are the railway people going to prevent them?"

The railway companies are what is known as "common carriers," and, in virtue of that classification, are bound to accept as a passenger any person in possession of a ticket who comports himself in such a way that other passengers are not annoyed, and abides generally by the laws regulating railway travelling. The cardsharping fraternity are quite aware of this and take the fullest advantage of the latitude which the and give evidence against them on prosecution.

Up till recently the authorities would only deal with cardsharpers under the Gaming (Scotland) Act, 1869, in terms of which the maximum punishment was 60 days' imprisonment. Owing to the number of the gangs operating on the railways, and their dodges for escaping detection, it was a very difficult matter to secure convincing proof against these people, while the light sentences imposed tended to encourage rather than suppress the nefarious business.

A Salutary Lesson

In September, 1922, however, a gang travelling with a train from Perth went a step too far by assaulting and attempting to rob a passenger whom they had vainly endeavoured to get into their clutches. In this case sufficient evidence was obtained. They were subsequently brought before the High Court at Glasgow, and, on being con-guard had been in the van in the interval. It appeared to have simply vanished from right under the nose of that official.

As a matter of fact it did nothing of the kind. No fault whatever could be found with the guard or any other official concerned. All were quite faithful to their trust, and actually saw the bicycle safely out of their charge.

Where, then, did the missing machine go, and how? As to the "where" I discovered it waiting to be called for at a luggage office separated by the whole breadth of Scotland from its intended destination. But how? I discovered that too, but for the present it must remain my secret and that of my successors in office.

Suffice it to say that people who "know the ropes" and "the tricks of the trade" may, once they fall from grace, with the aid of a little assurance, accomplish almost anything.

Another article of this series will

This motor van was being driven along the Forrestfield-Caldercruix road, near Airdrie, on Tuesday, when it skidded and toppled down the embankment on to the L.N.E. Railway. A passenger train from Edinburgh to Glasgow came along just at the moment, and before the driver could draw up the engine crashed into the motor lorry, which was completely wrecked. The driver and vanboy were seriously injured.

HEROIC NURSE

Intervenes to Protect Woman

wife, three daughters, and a maternity nurse were in the house at the time.

Immediately Mackay entered he drew down the sleeve of his jacket over his hand and swept the dishes off all the shelves. He then picked up a pair of tongs, but the nurse got hold of him and took them from him.

He struck his wife a severe blow on the face with his fist, kicked her on the body

Alexander Lang was held in great esteem by the men who know him, as shown by this souvenir, presented to him on the occasion of his retirement.

Chapter Two

THE
DETECTIVES

THE ORIGINS OF THE CRIMINAL INVESTIGATIONS DEPARTMENT

The Metropolitan Police were the first to form a 'Detective Police' department in 1842, a forerunner of the Criminal Investigations Department (CID); but there was an evident need for detectives on the railways, too. With an expanding railway network, carrying goods, passengers and their luggage, an increasing amount of theft took place. By 1849 six of the main companies were losing around £100,000 of property every day. Compensation claims began pouring in. David Stevenson, Goods Manager for the LNWR at Euston, wrote in 1853:

'Thieves are pilfering the goods from our wagons to an impudent extent. We are at our wits end to find out the blackguards. Not a night passes without wine hampers, silk parcels, drapers boxes or provisions being robbed; and if the articles are not valuable enough they leave them about the station. A roll of chintz was found on the station this morning, of course mistaken at first sight for silk, but on tearing the paper the plunderer discovered it to be chintz and threw it away in disgust. I wish he would send in his claim for loss of time; he should be paid in full!'

Dramatic Station Arrest

CARDIFF MILKMAN TO BE CHARGED

On Wednesday morning several Great Western Railway detectives made a dramatic arrest in connection with the alleged theft of a quantity of milk, a form of crime which has been very prevalent of late.

The detectives were concealed on the roof of the Central Railway Station, and there saw what will be the subject of a charge at the police court, in which the defendant is a well-known dairyman named Harold Tucker.

It was not only petty theft that was rife: bigger robberies were also on the increase. The passing of the Railways (Conveyance of Mails) Act in 1838 required railways to carry Her Majesty's Mail as the Postmaster General directed. This was very tempting for thieves, and a number of railway robberies followed suit. One of the most famous took place in 1849 when two thieves managed to rob the Up and Down Exeter Mail trains on the same day. The Up train arrived at Bridgewater at 10.30 p.m., where it was discovered that all the money, registered letters and parcels had been stolen. Later the same day, a similar discovery was made on the Down train which had left London for Bridgewater the previous evening. Two immaculately dressed first class passengers were arrested for the crime, having been seen 'acting suspiciously' by fellow passengers.

Some professional criminals went so far as to join the railway services to get inside information, and a number of thefts were committed by railway staff in collusion with outsiders. In 1873 ten railway men were sentenced to ten years imprisonment for stealing from their employers.

As crime patterns developed, so Parliamentary Acts were introduced to empower officers to deal with them. A number of Private Acts were passed to deal with track damage and thefts of stores, and the Regulation of Railways Acts of 1840 and 1842 and the Railway Clauses Act of 1845 provided powers for dealing with general crimes. Changes to legislation in 1861 meant that serious offences were prosecuted under the Offences Against the Persons Act and the Malicious Damage Act.

In the early days, detective work was carried out by senior uniformed officers – former Chief of Police Superintendent Collard of the Great Western Railway, for example, had been retained for such work after his official retirement in 1859. Freight thefts were sometimes investigated by Railway Clearing Houses, which regulated inter-company traffic rates, but these proved ineffective in dealing with difficult cases. To deal with an alarming increase in freight thefts, the London & North Western took the initiative of deploying officers disguised as porters to infiltrate and investigate problem stations. Officers were also briefed to observe people who made large compensation claims against railway companies for injuries supposedly gained on or around the railway, but who miraculously recovered after leaving court!

In 1863 the LNWR became the first Railway to create its own detective department. With its own chain of command, the department comprised a number of officers who worked separately to the uniformed Railway Police. At the turn of the century the detective and uniformed departments were reorganised into a more structured and integrated Force. The total strength, under a Chief of Police, was 350 men.

In 1864 the GWR was compelled to follow the London & North Western's lead. Henceforward the company was '. . . empowered to swear in detective

STOLEN CHEST OF TEA

DETECTIVE'S EARLY MORNING CHASE.

At a special Court on Friday, before Messrs David Williams and H. W. Thomas on the bench, two Kidwelly men, David Arnold Davies and Henry Williams (on bail), were charged with stealing a chest of tea, the property of the G.W.R. Co.—Mr. T. R. Ludford appeared to prosecute, and Mr. W. Davies defended.

P.C. Watts, of the G.W.R. police, who gave evidence on the previous occasion, stated that he kept observation on the men from a van, and after seeing them open a van door and take away the chest of tea, he came out, and the men ran away. Davies was overtaken, and accompanied witness to the signal-box. The other police officer took charge of the tea.

Cross-examined: He never threatened Davies with violence. When witness caught him, he had a boil on his arm, which witness re-bandaged.

Re-examined: He had no doubt as to the identity of the two men. Williams had a light grey waistcoat and a cap. He saw a similar coat when he called on Williams.

VAN ENTERED.

Arthur James King, a detective officer in the employ of the G.W.R. Co., stated that when the Neath to Neyland goods train arrived at Kidwelly at 2.30 a.m., he was on the train, on special duty. The two guards left the guards van, and proceeded towards the goods shed. The front portion of the train was detached, and taken towards the goods shed, and the remainder of the train stood on the down main line. Witness kept watch on the near-side. Two men came towards the waggons, and the doors of a van were opened. Witness was then in the guard's van, the length of six vans away.

officers when desirable.' Application to join the 'Special Police Department' (known as such to distinguish it from the uniformed traffic police) had to be made to Mr James Saunders, the Officer In Charge at Paddington. Recruits were drawn from the uniformed men and other railway grades, and, unlike the traffic police, were sworn in as Special Constables. They were paid at a slightly higher rate than the uniformed men and, in effect, performed practically all of the 'real' police work for the company. Even into the 1950s the South Western division of the British Transport Police retained the initials 'SP' (Special Police) as their departmental reference.

Ten years after the formation of the GWR Special Police Department, 70 cases had been successfully dealt with, and in time this grew to hundreds of convictions for theft every year.

Frith's 'The Railway Station' (1866) showing two plain-clothes detectives (Haydon and Brett) arresting a criminal at Paddington Station.
Courtesy of Felix Rosenstiel's Widow & Son Ltd.

Interestingly, it was in 1864, on 9th July, that the Railway Police recorded the first murder to take place on railway property. The culprit was a German named Müller who robbed and killed fellow passenger Thomas Briggs, Chief Clerk of a bank in Lombard Street, London. The man had been found beside the track and died of his wounds in hospital the following day.

With less detective experience than the Metropolitan Police, the Railway Police seconded experienced Metropolitan Detectives to lead their departments. These arrangements were to prove disastrously counter-productive in 1875 when the Metropolitan Police offered the services of one John Meiklejohn to the Midland Railway. Having taken charge of the detective branch in Derby, Meiklejohn was himself arrested on a number of fraud charges, as were a number of senior officers at Scotland Yard. Meiklejohn was convicted at the Old Bailey for 'conspiracy to defeat the ends of justice', which created a huge scandal and did much to discredit the Metropolitan Detective service. This misfortune was exacerbated when, in 1881, George Holmes, an officer on secondment to the London, Brighton & South Coast Railway handled a murder case so badly – the second on the railways – that a public statement was issued by Scotland Yard to the effect that they were disowning him, despite the fact that they continued to pay his salary.

Of course, these were the exceptions to the rule. In general, detectives played an important and integral role in the work of the Railway Police.

Evening Despatch

Telegrams: " Express," Birmingham.
Telephones: Central **3730** (five wires).

WEDNESDAY, 4 JULY, 1917.

LEAKING LEMONADE JAR.

SHUNTER WHO "CAUGHT THE DROPPINGS" FINED FOR THEFT.

At Birmingham to-day James Henry Hardwick, shunter, aged 26, of 61, Bacchus-road, was charged with stealing half-a-pint of essence of lemonade, value 1s., the property of the Great Western Railway Co., while in transit from Hockley to Bilston.

According to the evidence of G.W.R. Detectives Davies and King at midnight last night they heard movements inside a box truck in a siding at Hockley Goods Station, and got under the truck to await developments. They heard somebody moving about the van, and a little later a man with a lamp got out and walked away. A voice was heard calling out: " Look out, here's the —— d's," and Davis and King then saw the man, who proved to be the prisoner, throw away the contents of a drinking-can he was carrying. They stopped him and asked what he was doing in the truck, and he replied: " My fore-man will tell you."

Afterwards prisoner declared it was not him in the van, and that he put the can under the truck to catch the stuff that was leaking. Investigation revealed the fact that there was a stone jar of essence of lemonade in the van, and that prisoner's can had also contained lemonade.

Prisoner stated that he reported to his foreman that the van in question was leaking, and the foreman lent him his lamp to investigate. He did not take the can into the van with him as he had placed it under the van and picked it up when he got out of the van. He did not see the detectives till they stopped him.

Harry M. Smith, acting capstan fore-man, 124, Rosefield-road, Smethwick, corroborated, and added that he was on the way to report the condition of the contents of the van to the superintendent when prisoner called him back. He returned, and Detective Davis accused him of taking the cork from a bottle and pilfering the contents of whiskey inside it. Davis told him that both he and Hardwick would have to go to Kenyon-street Police Station, but after he had given his explanation to the superintendent he heard nothing more of it.

Detective-inspector Collins said it was scandalous the quantity of spirits and other goods that had been missed from Hockley Goods Station. Prisoner, however, had a clean sheet, and he did not associate him with the other thefts.

The Stipendiary (Lord Ilkeston) said he was satisfied prisoner stole the lemonade, although he did not tamper with the jar. It was a serious offence, for which he might very well be sent to prison. A fine of 60s. was imposed, prisoner being allowed 10 days to pay.

In 1894 historian John Pendleton paid tribute to them:

> 'The men in the Detective Departments on the railway do not fall like the persons they track, into disgrace. They are patient, enduring, smart and sometimes do clever and important work that has more money value to the company.'

DETECTIVE SERGEANT ROBERT KIDD

One detective who deserves particular note is Robert Kidd, the first Railway Policeman to be murdered in the course of his duties. Born in 1858, Kidd served in the City of Manchester Police before joining the London & North Western Railway Police in 1885. Four years later he was promoted to Detective Sergeant at Manchester Liverpool Road Station, dealing in the main with thefts of goods in transit, and of those stored in yards and sidings. On 29th September 1895, he and Detective Constable William Osbourne of Wigan were assigned to observe a goods yard at Wigan Station, the frequent target of raiders. The two officers arrived at the station around eight o'clock in the evening and made towards the sidings, whereupon they separated to begin patrol.

Shortly afterwards Osbourne spotted a man on his hands and knees and immediately challenged him as to his purpose. The man, who was later identified as William Halliwell, took off, calling out to his accomplices as he did so. Osbourne caught up with Halliwell, but was immediately set upon by two other men. Fearing he was about to be stabbed, he struck one of the men with his truncheon. Both men ran off into the night, but Osbourne then found himself being attacked by Halliwell with his own truncheon. For a few moments he lost consciousness and by the time he had recovered, Halliwell had disappeared. Osbourne got to his feet and staggered off in search of Kidd, eventually finding his colleague in a pool of blood between the wagons and a wall. He dragged Kidd up and carried him as far as a guard signal box where he alerted another colleague. A locomotive picked the two men up and took them to the passenger station; but it was too late for Kidd. The post-mortem revealed he had suffered nine stab wounds to the face and neck, with other cuts and abrasions to his body, including the severing of part of his left index finger. Some of these injuries were thought to have been inflicted after Kidd has lost consciousness. A subsequent search of the station yard revealed only one missing item – a jar of sweets.

Detective Sergeant
Robert Kidd

ELOPING WITH FRENCHMAN.

Dramatic Cardiff Station Scene.

HOW GIRL WAS SAVED BY DETECTIVE.

The chief characters in a remarkable story of an elopement which was stopped in the nick of time at Cardiff railway station are a Cardiff railway detective, a Frenchman, and an 18-year-old girl of exceedingly attractive appearance.

The Cardiff railway detective who was instrumental in preventing the elopement would at first be thought the villain of the piece for interfering with the course of true love, but had it not been for his masterly handling of the situation the girl would no doubt by now be reported missing, and all sorts of theories would be advanced as to what had happened to her.

The investigation into the murder was carried out by Wigan Borough Police and the County Police, who were later joined by Chief Inspector Richards (LNWR Manchester) and Superintendent Copping (LNWR Euston). Seven known suspects were quickly arrested for Kidd's murder, and three were charged: William Halliwell, Elijah Winstanley and William Kersley. In the Magistrates Court on 10th October, no less than 15 Justices sat to hear the charges. With both regional and national newspapers covering the story, Kidd's murder attracted massive public interest and large crowds gathered to hear the three defendants committed to trial.

Two months later, the accused appeared before Liverpool Winter Assizes before Mr Justice Collins. The jury in due course delivered a verdict of wilful murder against Kearsley and Winstanley, but all charges against Halliwell, who had given evidence against the other two, were dropped. Kearsley and Winstanley were sentenced to hang; Kearsley's sentence was commuted to penal servitude for life; and Winstanley was hanged on 17th December at Walton Gaol.

Robert Kidd died leaving a young wife and seven children. His death was a violent, tragic waste of life that symbolised the risk policemen must so often take in the execution of their duties. In his memory, an accommodation block at the Force Training School, Tadworth, has been named after him.

Chapter Three

THE LONDON UNDERGROUND

Between 1800 and 1850 the population in the capital doubled and London found itself becoming a victim of its own success. Every day some three quarters of a million people travelled throughout the crowded streets, on foot or on one of seven thousand horse-drawn vehicles – omnibuses, coaches, hackney carriages and drays, not to mention cattle, all vying with each other to reach their destinations. In the early 1850s Charles Pearson, a City solicitor, suggested that an underground railway might help relieve the congestion and Parliament agreed: a Select Committee of the House of Commons was appointed and in 1855 made recommendations that an underground railway should be built to connect the main line stations sited on the perimeters of the City.

The first proposals for the Metropolitan Railway were 'to encircle the Metropolis with a tunnel to be in communication with all the railway termini, thereby avoiding public congestion in the streets'. A further six years were to pass, however, before construction began using a part-tunnelling and part-'cut and cover' method, which entailed digging huge trenches, lining them with brickwork and then roofing them over, allowing the streets to be relaid above. Two and a half years later, on 10th January 1863, the world's first underground railway was officially opened to the public, becoming an instant success. Within three weeks, Myles Fenton (later knighted), the Metropolitan Railway's first General Manager, received a query from the manager of White's Club – 'To save further heavy wagering within the precincts of the club, the manager would be grateful if you would tell him what became of the earth removed from the tunnels.' The reply was – 'Go to *** Chelsea, and see for yourself!' It is doubtful whether any of the thousands of supporters regularly packing the Stamford Bridge ground of Chelsea Football Club realise that they are standing on soil excavated from the tunnels of the world's first underground railway.

For a short while the line operated on the old broad gauge system, but then, following the example of many new railways, on behalf of the Metropolitan, the Great Western Railway converted it to the standard 4 feet 8.5 inches. Steam engines were also provided by the GWR, and up until 1933, when the Metropolitan became part of the London Passenger Transport Board, there was a close working relationship between the two Companies. The new line ran between Farringdon and Bishops Road, Paddington, and, jointly with GWR, was subsequently extended to Hammersmith, with a branch to Addison Road (Olympia) known as the Hammersmith and City Line. In addition to passenger services, the GWR ran goods trains to Smithfield Meat Market and on to the Southern Railways.

From the beginning it was apparent that police officers would need to play a significant role in London's Underground. Trains were powered by steam which caused the atmosphere to become dank and dirty, and the dim gas lighting provided ideal conditions in which criminals could flourish. The Metropolitan Railway and the District Railway Companies already employed small police forces, and as each new part of the Underground system was built, so Parliamentary powers were granted and Magistrates given the authority to swear in Constables to police them. Officers were awarded authority over railway property and in respect of any offence which affected the railway, such as stone throwing or the causing of an obstruction. When required, assistance was given by Constables of the Metropolitan and City of London forces who were paid for services carried out on the company's behalf: 1s.6d. for removing a drunk or undesirable trespasser, and a further 1s.6d. if the case went to court. Constables employed by the Metropolitan Railway Company were fortunate in receiving main line (GWR) rates of pay and conditions of service.

As with the main line forces, Constables were recruited from the Armed Forces and also from within the railway organisation itself. Training was provided at the Railway's own training school at White City in respect of railway operation, and by an ex-Metropolitan Police Inspector in respect of police subjects. Officers' duties included making arrests, taking prisoners to the appropriate police station and signing charge sheets.

Accident at Earls Court. The Railway Policeman can be seen administering first aid to injured passengers.

Earls Court Station, 1876.

At the time of this photograph – one of the oldest to be found of a London Transport policeman – underground trains were still being hauled by steam locomotives.

A milestone in the history of the Force was the first overseas arrest by English police officers in 1874. Chief Inspector Gosden of the Metropolitan Railway Police and Inspector Littlechild of the Metropolitan Police Commissioner's Office travelled to Philadelphia via New York to arrest the English secretary and treasurer of the Metropolitan Railway Provident Savings Bank, Mr Tapson, who had absconded following a misappropriation of some £10,000. In 1940 the London Transport Police were to deal with a similar incident involving the same bank and a man in the same position, although this time the rogue was found closer to home, in the West Country, by Detective William Sweeting.

Chapter Four

POLICING
THE
DOCKS
AND
INLAND
WATERWAYS

THE CUT RUNNERS

The completion of the Bridgewater Canal in 1761 had heralded a new era for the transportation of goods, along with new opportunities for those who made their living by thieving. By far the most common crime on the waterways was pilfering, eventually prompting, in 1840, the passing of the Canals (Offences) Act which empowered navigation companies to appoint their own police officers to 'prevent depredations and robberies' and to control trespass by 'undesirables'. At this time only Sharpness Dock and the Aire & Calder Canal had anything resembling a police force to patrol their waterways; but the Act led a number of canals to establish their own, including the Grand Junction Canal, Regents Canal, the Shropshire Union Canal & Railway, the Leeds & Liverpool Canal and the St Helens Canal & Railway. With the exception of the Leeds & Liverpool Canal, all were to remain in force until nationalisation a hundred-odd years later. For reasons that cannot be traced, the latter was disbanded by the Water Committee in 1851.

Whilst many of the canal people were illiterate – constantly on the move it was impractical for children to attend school – they tended to be industrious and clean-living; therefore most of the incidents dealt with by 'Cut Runners' involved the factory employees who walked the towpaths on their way to and from work. In the dark, smog-filled evenings it was easy to slip among, and steal from, the boats' cargo stores – and even easier to slip into the canal itself. Pulling the victims of drowning, either accidental or suicide, from the murky waters was a common feature of a policeman's duties. The tunnel cutting near the Caledonian Road in London was a particularly notorious spot – so much so that at one time an average of 20 drown victims were being discovered every year. Eventually a house was built on the canal's edge and the first resident canal patrol was established, successfully reducing the death rate to one per year. The towpath between the Caledonian Road and Camden Road bridges was also a hotspot for thieves, who used it to enter and leave railway property at goods depots at York Way and St Pancras.

A London & Eirmingham Railway train passing over Regents Canal at Camden Town. The policeman observes.

A policeman's typical day included humorous incidents, too. In the days when canal boats were drawn by horse, one Sergeant A Waters described being called to the assistance of an extremely irate lady who was complaining that a certain barge-load was much too heavy for the horse and that Waters should report the boat's captain for cruelty to animals. In response, Waters pulled the barge himself for several yards, afterwards informing the lady that if he could pull it, the horse certainly could.

Under the Transport Act of 1947, by which time some 2,475 miles of inland waterways had been built, canals were nationalised to come under the jurisdiction of the 'British Transport Commission Police'.

Aire & Calder Navigation Police	c. 1826 –1.1.1948
Grand Union Canal Police	1.1.1929 – 1.1.1948
(i) Grand Junction Canal Police	c1840 – 1.1.1929
(ii) Regents Canal Police	c1840 – 1.1.1929
Lea Conservancy Police	u/k – 1.1.1948
Sharpness Dock Police	c1827 – 1.1.1948
Sheffield & South Yorkshire Navigation Police	1895 – 1.1.1948
Shropshire Union Railway & Canal Police	3.8.1846 – 27.7.1857
St Helens Canal & Railway Police	16.7.1846 – 29.7.1864

BUTES BOBBIES

During the 19th century many railway companies had an interest in the country's expanding docks, where railway installations, ships, equipment, warehouses and offices in the port area, all required policing. The Harbours, Docks and Piers Act of 1847 (Section 79) empowered two Justices to appoint Special Constables to cover the dock and harbour areas, and up to one mile outside them.

Work began on Cardiff's Bute Docks in 1835 and continued until 1907, by which time it had become the largest coal exporting port in the world. Teeming with seamen, longshoremen, coalers, victuallers, vagabonds, prostitutes and immigrants, the docklands became an increasingly lawless environment. The City Fathers, concerned about their effect on the town in general, proposed the formation of a private force, and in 1865 the Marquess of Bute was given authority to begin recruitment. The result – 'Butes Bobbies' – was one of the first and largest private police forces in the country, employing over 70 men at its peak. The officers wore green uniforms with gilt buttons and facings, and, in addition to the docks area, policed Cardiff Castle, the seate of the Marquess of Bath's family.

Butes Bobbies soon established a reputation that earned them respect. Dockland crime subsided within a few months, and rioting, formerly a regular occurrence, became almost non-existent. Part of this may be due to the fact that officers were permitted to carry sabres on patrol; but it was also due to the severity of sentences for those who dared cross them. A woman found soliciting could be given seven days hard labour, or, if 'riotously soliciting', 14 days; those charged with gambling received seven days hard labour or a ten shilling fine; whilst loiterers received three months imprisonment. Interestingly, in those pre-Ian Fleming days, a 'James Bond' appeared regularly in the punishment books, receiving sentences for rioting that varied between three and 18 months.

The Force took itself very seriously indeed and misdemeanours by the bobbies themselves were treated with equal severity. They were known to be lovers of 'strong waters', but to be found drunk on duty not surprisingly resulted in dismissal. One Constable who was found with 'hands in pockets with the skirts of his great coat apart', compounded his crime by having the audacity to play snow-balls with a customs officer. His frivolous behaviour lost him a day's pay. Constables who were spotted on the streets when they were receiving sick pay would have their wages deducted for five weeks. One Welsh port Superintendent reported that officers he considered to be perfectly contented had recently requested one day off in seven. His response had been to threaten them with their jobs if they pursued the matter any further!

*Butes Bobbies,
c. 1892-1904.*

Early in the 1920s the Forces of Barry Railway Company, Swansea
Harbour Trust and Bute Docks amalgamated with the Great Western
Railway. The GWR Annual Report of 1923 provides an interesting
summary of the prosecutions and other work carried out by its docks
police:

	No of incidents
Larceny	63
Drunkenness	31
Strikes & lock-outs	1
Disturbances on board ships	4
Assaults on police	1
Persons sleeping out without viable means	5

Petty offences – gaming, trespassing, bathing, etc.	80
Rescued from docks	8
Found drowned	7
Fires	9
Women on docks (ill-renown or dubious morals)	28
Breaking and entering	22
Illness on docks	16
Boats & vessels adrift in the docks	10
Spillage of water (pressure pipes bursting)	16
Insecure premises	190
Damage to property	64
Suicide on board ships	2
Inquests	16
Electric lights out	860
Property lost	30
Welding cars on the dock premises	85
Offences under the Betting Acts	2
Boys and children found on docks	47
Spillages of oil at Queens Dock	19
Persons afflicted with mental derangement on board ships etc & police rendered necessary assistance in affecting their removal to a mental institution.'	4
Imported dogs	10
Persons infracting the National Oil Refineries Rules & Regs	15
Persons trading on docks without a license	8
Persons detected removing contraband goods from vessels with the intention of evading duty	10
Political meetings held on docks	1
Indecent exposure	20

    – 'including 10 unmarried couples who violated the laws of decency by exposing themselves whilst in the act of sexual intercourse within the view of the public'

Gross indecency by male persons	3
Goods leaving docks without a pass	34
Irregularities committed by marine-store dealers	4
Accidents on docks	180
First aid cabinets in use	500

Sergeant of the Barry Docks Police, South Wales, with canine posing (ahead of its time) as a police patrol dog.
Courtesy of South Wales Police Museum

Police Constable Brown between 1908 and 1914.

Hull & Barnsley police at the main entrance to Alexandra Dock, c. 1900

GOOLE DOCKS

Under the jurisdiction of Humber Ports Division came Goole Docks, which has an interesting and unusual history of policing. In 1864 the Directors of the Aire & Calder Navigation Company, who owned the docks and many West Riding canals, resolved that it was

> ' . . . desirable to make arrangements for the better watching of the docks at Goole and that the Directors will be ready to join with the Lancashire and Yorkshire Railway Company at the expense of obtaining the services of the County Constabulary.'

As a result, one Constable of the Yorkshire West Riding Constabulary was appointed to the docks. (Under Section 19 of the County Police Act of 1840, a Constable additional to the ordinary establishment could, on request, be appointed for duty on private premises if the Chief Constable considered it desirable and the police authority approved.) The Lancashire & Yorkshire Railway were involved because they had extensive interests in the docks; they would have preferred to employ their own police; but as they did not own the docks it was impossible for them to do so.

In 1881 the average maintenance cost for one Constable was 24/6d per week. The continued industrial growth and expansion of the premises combined with the improvement in police conditions of service to increase the size of the establishment to six officers in 1913. The cost, by now £700 per annum, continued to be jointly borne; however, because the Lancashire & Yorkshire had taken over the 23 vessel Goole Steam Shipping Company, they agreed to meet 45% of the total sum. Despite the Lancashire & Yorkshire's subsequent amalgamation and eventual nationalisation, the arrangements remained in effect through to 1953, by which time police costs exceeded £3,500 a year.

In 1884 the Aire & Calder Navigation Company obtained powers to appoint Special Constables to act on their property and up to a quarter of a mile therefrom. The Constables were empowered to enter any boat lying in the docks or canals if they suspected that an offence was taking place, arrest suspects and recover suspected stolen property. These Special Constables were not full time policemen: they were employees of the Aire & Calder Navigation Company who continued in their ordinary occupations and undertook to perform police work only when necessary. A 'roll of Special Constables' was still in existence in the late 1930s and staff listed received a quarterly payment in recognition – 30 shillings for Constables and a little more for Sergeants and those of higher rank. It is probable that these Special Constables performed only a limited range of police work and were necessary to supplement the under-manned West Riding policemen. In particular, their presence would have been important along the canals which stretched many miles, and through sparsely populated areas. So far as it is known, they did not wear uniform at first, although in the fullness of time they received full Special Constable's dress.

SOUTHAMPTON DOCKS

The Southampton Dock Company was formed in 1836, with construction work beginning two years later. As with the railways the construction site required some measure of protection and at least two uniformed watchmen were employed. As the size of the docks grew, so the number of Constables was increased. In 1872 the Directors of the Dock Company issued the very first police instructions book which laid down such principles as preserving law and order, protecting life and property, and guarding against fire.

As the docks steadily grew in importance many changes became necessary. In 1892 the London & South Western Railway Company took over Southampton Docks together with its police force of one

Inspector, three Sergeants, 11 uniformed Constables, and two plain clothes Constables. All officers were re-sworn in as Constables of the London & South Western Railway, and in so doing not only enjoyed the powers, privileges and protections of a Constable of that Force, but also extended their jurisdiction to embrace the railway lines and premises of the latter company.

Officers at Southampton Docks,
c. 1890s.

c. June 1938.

Chapter Five

THE
WAR YEARS
AND
BETWEEN

WORLD WAR I – 'THE SPECIALS'

When war broke out in 1914, few people believed it would last anywhere near as long as four years. Within a few months vast numbers of troops were being mobilised to dispatch the 'enemy', placing enormous pressure on the civilian forces who had to maintain the country in a semblance of order. The Midland Railway Police lost 152 of its 272 uniformed staff to the Colours (of whom 27 were later killed and 38 wounded); whilst one third of all North Eastern Railway officers were called to arms, forming a whole 'Kitchener's' battalion – the Northumberland Fusiliers. The North Eastern Railway owned workshops which manufactured huge quantities of munitions for the front and many of the NER men who remained at home were in demand by Government departments.

As the scale of the War was realised, so control of the railways was taken over by the Government through a Railway Executive Committee which could oversee the transporting of raw materials to munitions factories, and shells, guns and troops to the ports. The Executive identified a need for extra police officers and, to answer that need, it was decided to raise a Special Constabulary within the Metropolitan Police District, the members of which would guard points in their own time. Within two weeks 20,000 men had joined, taken the oath and were available for duty. At its peak the Metropolitan Special Constabulary (MSC) had 24,000 men on its strength.

In addition, the London General Omnibus Company, the Post Office, Office of Works, and numerous public utility companies such as gasworks were permitted to raise detachments of 'Specials' from their employees to defend their own premises. Only the LGOC detachment were permitted to perform general duty on raid nights and, unlike the other Special Constables, were provided with a uniform.

A Caledonian police officer with a group of troops.

Some railway companies also selected railwaymen as Special Constables. When air raids threatened, the men put on police armlets and took up duty around the station to assist the company's regular policemen in controlling the crowds or whatever other duties were necessary. During air raids the Great Eastern Railway Company's Chief of Police took charge of both regular and Special Police at Liverpool Street Station. A bomb was later to fall on Liverpool Street Station in a daylight raid, killing 16 and wounding 13; whilst a raid on St Pancras Station resulted in the deaths of 20 people. Whether these 'Specials' were sworn in under the Special Constables Act of 1831 or under the companies' own acts, which contained sections authorising the appointment of Police, is not known. Special Constables were also enrolled at Goole Docks, to guard vulnerable points against sabotage by enemy agents. This duty was to be carried out in their spare time and was unpaid.

Policewomen of the North Eastern Railway at Darlington, c. 1915.

To help alleviate the problems of chronic under-staffing at Middlesborough, Darlington, Newcastle and York Railways, the first women volunteers were employed. They patrolled the stations and goods warehouses in pairs, being paid approximately two-thirds of the men's wages. Other local police forces also began to employ women to patrol large railway stations and naval or military establishments in an effort to protect the morals of young girls attracted there by servicemen.

THE RAILWAYS ACT OF 1921

By the time hostilities had ended in 1918, hundreds of young Railway Police officers had been tragically killed or wounded and a number of major recruitment drives had to be initiated, the most notable being Captain Horwood's of the North Eastern Railway which, amongst other things, offered sports clubs, annual gala days and social evenings! It was not too difficult to build numbers up again, as many ex-servicemen were now looking for gainful employment in disciplined, uniformed organisations. In addition, nation-wide railway police rates of pay were being improved and standardised, although remaining lower than Home Office police rates of pay; and, since the turn of the century, the principal companies had been re-organising their forces so that menial tasks were removed from the list of duties. Police officers were now solely employed to (1) prevent and detect crime; and (2) maintain law and order on the railway undertakings.

Also in 1918 was the unification of the Great Western Railway Special and Traffic Police into one body under Mr J H Matthews who had been the company's senior Detective officer since 1912. In fact the amalgamation had been advocated for many years, with other Railway Companies carrying out their unifications as early as the first few years of the 20th century. Not all of the uniformed men could meet the improved standards of the newly organised Force, but those who did were sworn in, granted standard rates of pay and, for the first time, came under a purely police determined chain of command. Chief of

Police Matthews was the first of three persons to hold that post. He was succeeded in 1936 by Mr George Stephens who, in turn, was succeeded ten years later by Mr Arthur Lane, who held office at the time of the 1947 Transport Act and nationalisation.

By 1921 the strength of the principal railway Police Forces (including supervisors) was as follows:

	Staff	*Supervisors*
Caledonian Railway	76	4
Great Central Railway	214	12
Great Eastern Railway	301	21
Great Northern Railway	290	14
Great Western Railway	333	33
Lancashire & Yorkshire Railway	121	11
London, Brighton & South Coast Railway	137	8
London & North Western Railway	354	46
London & South Western Railway	213	13
Midland Railway	318	14
North Eastern Railway	414	14
North British Railway	145	10
Metropolitan Railway	3	3
South Eastern & Chatham Railway	161	11

Total Staff 3,080

Only 20 of the 120 or so railway companies had an official police department, and the different forces varied enormously in organisation, policies, duties and standards. It seemed more sensible and economic to group the Railway companies into four main lines, and thus, from 1924, following the 1921 Railways Act, they were as follows:

The Great Western Railway	335 officers
The London Midland & Scottish Railway (LMSR)	790 officers
The London & North Eastern Railway (LNER)	1,360 officers
The Southern Railway (SR)	510 officers

The three latter companies incorporated at least three major constituent companies each, and a very unsettled period of redundancies and redeployment followed. Each new force came under the control of a Chief of Police, and comprised a number of divisions. Divisions were commanded by a Superintendent and comprised districts in the charge of an Inspector or Sergeant. LMS, SR and GWR Headquarters were established at their respective London terminals; whilst LNER Headquarters were at London and York. Both uniformed and detective officers were sworn in as Constables and with the exception of the GWR, the word 'Special' was dropped from their title. GWR officers were also the only Force to wear a crown in their badge, originally granted by Queen Victoria for services rendered. During the years 1923 and 1926 statutes were obtained which empowered the companies to appoint police officers on their own system, and widened the powers of their jurisdiction.

Although policing was steadily becoming more formalised, some odd duties remained. On the LMS one officer had the job of observing employees on sick leave to ensure that they were not malingering and another was required to feed and water the cartage horses on Sundays. On the Southern Railway, officers also acted as debt collectors, representing the legal department.

THE RAILWAY POLICE FEDERATION

1919 saw the first meeting of the Railway Police Federation, a body of men who could deal collectively with the rates of pay and conditions of service for the 14 Railway Police forces in existence at that time. Prior to this, officers had relied on their Chief of Police to represent them when dealing with the general manager and directors of the companies.

The historic meeting attended by Railway Police representatives which resulted in the setting up of the Railway Police Federation.

Back row (left to right): Sergeant Middleton (Great Central), PC Minns (Alexandra Dock and Railway), PC Maton (Cardiff Railway), PC J Kendall (Midland), PC J Mason (Great Eastern), Detective Sergeant J Wood (London & South Western).

Front row: Detective Fall (Lancashire & Yorkshire), Inspector R Garbutt (Great Northern), Inspector H John (Great Western), Inspector Dexter (London & Northern Western), Sergeant Reynolds (Great Western). In front, PC Robinson (North Eastern).

With the passing of the Railways Act of 1921, the Federation was put on a statutory basis which dictated that each company should establish a conference consisting of equal numbers of police and management representatives. Since this moment the Federation has striven to represent the officers wherever possible, often liaising with the Police Federation of England and Wales and those of other non-Home Office forces which, in 1995, includes forces from several European countries. Seventy-six years after the first meeting, the aims and objectives of the British Transport Federation are described thus:

1.	To secure and utilise the Machinery of Negotiation to improve conditions of service and to protect the interests of the membership.

2.	To assist members in disciplinary procedures ensuring that they are dealt with fairly during investigations and the provision of legal assistance where applicable.

3.	Through contact with the Parliamentary Representative to monitor the passage through Parliament of all relative legislation and ensure members conditions and positions are correct.

4.	Using recognised Machinery to ensure that the working environment is improved and that standards are maintained.

5.	Through the Welfare fund to give assistance to serving and retired members and their families in cases of unforeseen hardship.

6.	To assure the self continuance of the Federation and the provision of any other service which from time to time may be required.

Today the Federation is funded by subscription deducted from members' pay, and employs a Chairman, General Secretary and a part time administrator. As well as the more formalised duties it carries out on behalf of its members, it also runs a lottery for members, with large sums of money being donated to charities.

Conference of Chiefs of Police,
Brighton, 11th July 1922

THE GROWTH OF TRADE UNIONISM

Between World Wars the country hovered on the brink of its own civil war – between government, employers and trade unions. Trade unions had begun flexing their muscles in the early 1900s with an increasing number of disputes. Strikes had been held during 1910 and 1912 but conditions had not improved; and the three largest unions – the Miners, the National Transport Workers Federation (NTWF) and the National Union of Railwaymen (NUR) – had joined together to create the Triple Alliance. This alliance proved effective in its work against the immediate post-World War I government control of railways and mines; however, when control was handed back in 1921, miners, railwaymen and dockers all received pay cuts. In the dispute that followed, the Triple Alliance fell apart. The problem was exacerbated when the Samuel Report of 1926 recommended further cuts in wages, with no increase in working hours. The mine owners refused to accept this and a lock-out followed suit. After cabinet talks fell apart a National Strike was called, with workers in transport, iron and steel, electricity, gas, building and newspaper printing all taking part. The Strike threatened the country's life lines and Special Constables and volunteers, issued with identification cards, again had to be employed to assist in protecting track and railway property. Railway Police found themselves walking the tracks to check for obstructions, just as their predecessors had done nearly one hundred years before. There were fears that the Strike would continue for a long time, but fortunately the TUC called it off after only nine days. The miners remained 'locked-out' for a further seven months, and were forced to return on their employers' terms.

Following the strike, life for the Railway Police settled down to a relatively peaceful phase. In his Annual Report for 1931, the Chief of Police of the North Eastern Railway noted that the 2,205 prosecutions made that year were a significant decrease in the number of the previous year. He remarked:

> 'It is gratifying to know there is less crime on the railway today than there was in pre-war times, particularly having regard to the distress prevalent in industrial areas and the large army of unemployed.'

CHIEF GENERAL MANAGER,
LONDON & NORTH EASTERN RAILWAY
KING'S CROSS STATION,
N.1.

P.C. ___ Marshall.   May 15th – 1926

Dear Sir,

I wish to take the first possible opportunity of conveying a special message of thanks to the members of the staff who have stood by the Company during the strike which is now happily at an end.

It has been a very great achievement, on which we may all congratulate ourselves, and for which, on behalf of the Company, I thank you all.

Believe me

Yours very truly

R. L. Wedgwood

One Constable described his duties at Liverpool Street Station in a 1935 issue of the *London and North Eastern Railway Magazine*:

'I am 6.0 a.m. and 2.0. p.m. duty and booked West Side patrol on the duty roster. I have relieved the officer on night duty and he has reported "all correct", but I must have a good look round in case some careless person has left some luggage or parcels unattended since my colleague passed that way.

Quite a crowd off the boat train this morning, most of them foreigners, diamond merchants, wool buyers, etc. I must keep a sharp look out here, as this is where some of the best pickpockets and confidence tricksters get to work, but I can see two detectives on the platform so I can safely leave it to them. Here comes a gentleman in trouble, this is more in my line; a German by his appearance but he can speak English. "I cannot find my luggage, officer; what am I to do?" he asks.

A lady next approaches me. "Oh! officer I have left a fox fur somewhere in this train, shall I be able to find it again?" "Certainly, madam, that is if no dishonest person has found it first" is my reply.

By this time the second boat train is in, 8.30. a.m. Everybody is in a hurry. "The quickest way to Paddington?" – "How do I get to Hatton Garden officer?" – "Where do I get a taxi?" – "Can you find my porter officer?" – I answer all these and a dozen other questions, at the same time I am seeing that no luggage is taken out of the guard's van, without a registration ticket being given up for it, but everything works smoothly this morning, and I get no complaints.

There is a large crowd for the 9.52 Yarmouth and the Flushing trains. I start the queue for the Yarmouth first, they want a bit of sorting out, quite a few here for intermediate stations and their train goes from the East Side, so I call out "Yarmouth only on this queue".

The queues at Nos. 7, 8 and 9 platforms are by this time fairly lengthy and I have all my work cut out seeing that passengers do not join the wrong line and keeping gangways clear.

A guard comes up to me holding a little boy by the hand. "He was handed to me at Halesworth," says the guard, "and his mother is supposed to meet him; it is half an hour since my train arrived and nobody has come to claim him yet, will you take charge of him?" I then question the little chap. "How old are you, son, and where do you live?" I find out he is ten years old and resides at Deptford. Further questions elicit the fact that a No. 78 bus passes his home, but he has got no money. All right, I haven't time to look after him for long, so out into the street we go to the bus stop, ask the conductor to put him off at his home, and pay his fare. (If I had put all the money I have spent this way during my service at Liverpool Street Station, I should be able to buy that radiogram I saw last week).

In conclusion, I do not want readers to think this is all a police officer has to do at Liverpool Street Station. If I were to give in detail all the cases in which an officer may be called upon to act during an ordinary eight-hour turn of duty, I should require a book as large as *The Seven Pillars of Wisdom.*'

PC J Carter, 78W, amongst a sea of umbrellas at the Lost Property Office of LNER, Farringdon Road in 1930. Every one of them was scanned by police officers for addresses before being sold.

THE LONDON PASSENGER TRANSPORT BOARD ACT OF 1933

In 1933 an Act of Parliament created the London Passenger Transport Board, responsible for all the non-main line railways in London. A domestic enquiry followed to decide on policing policy and concluded that the Board should maintain its own Force: it was subsequently granted statutory authority for Magistrates to appoint Constables to police its premises. Under the terms of the new legislation, Superintendent Percy Smith of the Metropolitan Railway Police took command of all the company's police and security units that had been absorbed by the new Board, with the exception of the London County Council Tramways. The following establishment was authorised:

Superintendent	1
Deputy Superintendent	1
Executive Assistant	1
Clerks	2
Detective Chief Inspector	1
Detective Inspectors	2
Uniform Inspectors	1
Detective Sergeants	4
Uniform Sergeants	2
Detective Constables	12
Women Detective Constables	2
Uniform Constables	28
Women Uniform Constables	1
Testers (Fraud)	2
Civil –	
Chief Ticket Inspector	1
Foreman Inspectors	2
Travelling Ticket Inspectors	32

95

*Three police cap badges worn by London Transport
Police officers, showing both the King and the Queen's Crown.*

Courtesy of Brian Deacon

LONDON PASSENGER TRANSPORT
BOARD POLICE.

This is to certify that I, one of the
Magistrates of the Police Courts of the
Metropolis have, on the application of
the London Passenger Transport Board
pursuant to the powers in that behalf
vested in me by Section 107 of the London
Passenger Transport Act, 1934, appointed

Laurence Ryan

to act as one of the constables mentioned
in the said Act in and upon the property of
the Board as therein specified.

This is his authority for executing the
duties of that office.

One of the Magistrates of the Police Courts
of the Metropolis

Date of appointment ....

Signature
of Holder } *Patrick Ryan*

Warrant No. **198**

Alfred G Peedle, formerly Chief of Police London Transport Area and a Constable during the 1930s, described a typical Constable's day thus:

> 'Book on at Cranbourn Chambers [headquarters] at 6.30 am. Walk to Strand station and there turn out the tramps who went into the subways for warmth when the station opened. Then to Charing Cross Station to remove tramps sleeping on the station roof under the Southern Railway tracks. Onwards by train to Morden Station to assist in control of the heavy workmen's traffic. Cheap workmen's tickets were issued up to 7.30 am at which time the Constable and members of the station staff would take up positions at the end of the queues at the ticket windows. All late comers had to pay full fare. Leave Morden about 8 am, return to Leicester Square to report to the duty Sergeant at Cranbourn Chambers. This followed by a 30 minute refreshment break, then off to Oxford Circus and Tottenham Court Road Stations, or on Thursday and Friday to 55 Broadway to escort a paymaster, finishing duty not before 3 pm – a total of 8 hours 30 minutes.'

> *(Friends of London Transport Museum Newsletter)*

Constables worked 13 days out of 14, with Sundays paid extra at a day and a quarter. There was no sick pay or pension, and annual leave was limited to six days per annum. On promotion to Sergeant, however, officers enjoyed limited sick pay, a free holiday pass, and membership of the Railway Superannuation Fund.

As the new Force became established and respected, so the road services of buses, coaches and tramways began requesting assistance and special squads were set up to deal with them. As well as controlling passenger traffic in peak times, officers were required to police fans travelling to football matches at Waltham Green, Arsenal, Tottenham and Wembley; cricket matches at Lords and the Oval; and such special events as King George V's Jubilee, his lying in State at Westminster, and the Coronation of King George VI. All these events brought massive crowds into London, and in the limited confines of the Underground stations the police were hard pressed to maintain order. As a result of stresses and strains particular to the capital city, from 1934 onwards *all* railway supervisory staff were sworn in as Special Constables.

WORLD WAR II

When World War II broke out, Britain was instantly swept by 'invasion fever'. The belief that the country was in imminent danger of invasion by hostile forces – or, at the very least, major sabotage by enemy agents who were believed to be 'infiltrating' the country at every level – was widespread. Fortunately this fear proved relatively groundless but aircraft had developed considerably since the First War and air raids, signified by the siren that went off only seconds after Britain was declared officially 'at war', were to prove far more deadly. Indeed, for the Railway and Docks Police, all the problems of the First War were intensified in the Second – reduced numbers within the Forces, which had to be augmented by volunteer women and pensioners; increased high security risk areas; rising incidents of theft as a result of the rationing; and rising accident and crime rates due to the enforced nightly black-outs. Though a number of troops were retained for home defence, responsibility for railway bridges, reservoirs, telephone exchanges, power stations, etc., and the carriage of troops and supplies to the various ports – all of which were prime targets for German bombs – still fell upon the Railway and Docks Police.

Almost immediately after the declaration of war, the various police headquarters were evacuated to safer areas outside London, and control of the railway system was once again taken over by a Railway Executive Committee. The Chiefs of Police met regularly as a sub-committee to co-ordinate and direct the Forces, and they in turn reported back to the Executive Committee. Superintendent Smith of the newly formed London Transport Police was among them, responsible for the appointment of some 2,000 Special Constables.

In addition to his usual responsibilities, the Chief of Police of Great Western was appointed Air Raid Precautions Officer and Chief Fireguard for the company; and large numbers of temporary police had to be recruited to guard the docks and other 'Protected Places' and 'Vulnerable Points' on the system. In London 'Vulnerable Points' included the tube stations where bomb damage to sewers or water mains could cause major flooding. Charles Graves, author of *London Transport at War,* referred to the control unit which could automatically close the specially erected floodgates:

'The key to the collective control of all the flood gates was a small room with bronze doors in the passage between the Piccadilly and Northern Lines at Leicester Square. Thousands of people must have passed it every day without realising the immense importance of what occurred behind the back of the sturdy police Constable, sole safe-guard against sabotage.'

From the beginning of September to early February 1941, London was bombed every night, with raids often lasting from dusk till dawn. There were some 10,000 reported incidents on the railways alone. One such report, from Police Constable 105 V H Bampton to his superior officers, was printed in the BTP Journal of 1973. The old Great Northern Goods Depot, to which it refers, was situated in the shadow of the docks on the boundary between the City of London and the East End, and therefore one of the worst hit areas.

'At 10 pm 5 October I took over duty at Royal Mint Street. PC 106 G Asker took over Continental Gate. PC 153 F Eden was off duty sheltering in the Potato Arch. At 10.30 pm PC Asker and myself were by the Shunters Bunk near the old hoist, when a stick of bombs were released by an Enemy plane. The first gave us a bit of shock and we encouraged one another by repeating 'stand fast, stand fast'. This one was followed by at least three others quite close to us. When the air had cleared, Asker and I called out to PC Eden and finding that he was uninjured, we set out to investigate and noticed the following damage.

One HE Bomb had penetrated and shattered about three spans of the glass roof opposite the Middle Gate, usually called the "East Gate", and made a large crater, also practically the whole of the glass in the Depot including offices is broken. The majority of the doors of offices and cupboards were forced open by the blast. One wicket gate forced. West Gate seriously damaged. Signal box put out of action. Except for damaged window frames and broken glass and doors and cupboards already mentioned in accounts office, the whole of the warehouse is intact.

Another bomb dropped through the Midland Railway Bridge in Mansell Street making a large crater in the road, the force of the blast smashing the back road gates of Mint Street East Depot.

A third bomb fell in the road just outside the West Gate making a large crater, damaging the water and hydraulic mains.

A fourth bomb fell at the end of the Minories damaging the gas main and cutting off our gas supply.

We informed your P S Unwin at Bishopsgate by telephone and requested that he get in touch with you, Sir. We also informed the City and Metro Police that one bomb had dropped in the Depot, representatives of both forces visited the Depot.

From 11.30 5th October till 4 am 6th October your PC 153 Eden took over duty Mint Street East, while PC Asker and myself were making a search of the premises and lines.

Under the circumstances it is impossible for us to give a more detailed account of the material damage as during the whole of the time broken glass was falling about us.'

Yours Obediently,

PC 105 V H Bampton
PC 106 Geo Asker

*Policeman and Belgian
Nuns at Waterloo, 1940.*

Painting: Helen McKie,
NRM/Science & Society Picture Library

Fred Furness began working for LNER as a Constable in February 1939, and remained with the Force until retirement in May 1974. During the war years he was most often on nightshift (10.00 p.m. to 6.00 a.m.), and would leave his home in Potters Bar at 8 p.m. to catch a train into the City. Potters Bar is the highest point on the London to York line, and Furness recalls how one bright moonlit evening in the early part of the war, just as his train came 'chuffing' up the hill with a beautiful plume of smoke billowing out from its funnel, a 'Jerry' plane appeared in the sky. It swooped alarmingly low, dropping, as it did so, hundreds of incendiary devices over the area. At this time the incendiaries lacked sophisticated and simply burnt out, so that the event is remembered as a visual spectacle rather than as prelude to tragedy. However, over the years German anti-personnel devices became more and more deadly. Furness was later promoted to Inspector, in charge of a crime squad of six officers, and recalls how at 6.00 a.m., regular as clockwork, a V2 rocket would appear in the sky to wreak death 'and destruction on the City of London.

Officers coped well with the bombings on the job, but found it difficult to leave their loved ones at home, knowing that they were at risk and that tragedy in some form might await them on their return. The late shift men were often unable to get home because of the raids and had to spend the night in some relatively safe, but usually uncomfortable, part of the station where they worked; whilst the early shift men had to be up and at work at the usual time whatever the events of the night.

Fred Furness also recalls the volume of theft incidents – in fact, during the war years crime on the railways exceeded the total amount of crime recorded by all other British Police Forces put together. Thefts of light bulbs and other train fittings, and luggage and parcels from platforms, were of particular concern, as were the number of thefts of bicycles from stations by soldiers and airmen stranded some distance from their camps. These misadventures prompted Railway Police to lecture to the Army Special Investigation Branch at Aldershot and seek out the offenders! Furness and his men would be catching half a dozen criminals every evening, and having time for only one officer to escort them all to court the following morning.

In the minutes of the Railway Executive Police Committee of October 1943, an item was raised concerning the number of thefts and breakages of cups and saucers on trains, underlining the point that HM Forces appeared to be responsible for a great deal. In 1938 31,000 incidents occurred and in 1941, 554,000. By 1942 the figure had dropped to less than 250,000, said to be due to 'measures taken'.

The evacuation of over half a million children and expectant mothers from the city was a massive operation, and a triumph for all concerned. In just four days the children were safely conveyed from schools to railway stations, via the Underground system, to continue their journey on main lines into safer areas of the country. Police officers of the LPTB and main line Forces were on hand to marshall them through, their 'all in a day's work' duties extending to the provision of shoulders and handkerchiefs for the tearful parents and children to cry upon. It wasn't all doom and gloom: many of the younger evacuees had little understanding of what was happening and considered themselves to be embarking on a great adventure. Policewomen were employed, as well as Special Constables, to increase the staff numbers and proved highly suited for helping the children on their way. The first woman police officer to work at Kings Cross was Hetty Hinchley WI. In the LNER Journal of January 1943 P. Piper, the first policewoman on the London & North Eastern Railway, based at Liverpool Street Station tells how

> ' . . . The other day an evacuee decided to return to London and tried to pass through the barrier with only a rather dirty looking platform ticket, and when I asked him why he had done it, he said he was fed up with the country and wanted some life. All these children have to be looked after until friends or parents can be found.'

Helping evacuees on their way.

As well as evacuees, thousands of troops passed through the London stations on their way to the ports and airfields – in 1940 some 300,000 men embarked on 620 trains for the invasion of Dunkirk. Prisoners of war also passed through – officers recall being impressed by the immaculate tailoring and smartness of the Luftwaffes' uniforms, but not so by their owners' arrogance.

To the initial consternation of the Government, many Londoners took to using tube stations as air-raid shelters; they simply arrived and placed their bedding on the platforms. Recognising the logic of this, however, railway authorities made considerable moves to accommodate them. Regulations were drawn up, bunks erected, refreshment services arranged, toilets installed and First Aid posts manned. By the end of September 1940, 177,000 people sheltered in the deep level tube stations and by 1941 bunk beds were installed in 79 stations. Many people stayed underground for weeks on end.

Being underground did not guarantee safety. Railway terminals, both underground and main line, were common targets for German bombs, and officers' duties included the investigation of reports of unexploded bombs on railway property. On receiving a report, the officer would immediately effect temporary restrictions. He would (1) close the line; (2) authorise working of a single line; or (3) leave the line open but limit speed to five miles per hour. He would then travel to the scene of the bomb to assess its nature, whether it was a delayed-action, armour piercing or blast effect device, and determine the extent of the potential damage.

On 14th October 1944 disaster struck at Balham Station when a bomb fractured a sewer, and a water main broke into the tunnel. Within minutes the lower station, home to many shelters, was filled with sludge and water. Though some people managed to escape by running through the tunnel to the next station, the flood gates had been locked against them which cut off their main exit. A survivor and member of the Underground staff described the scene:

'I crawled through the emergency exit, shone my torch and had a shock when I saw a mountain of ballast, sand and water washing through a huge hole at the north end of the platform. The water was about two feet deep in the lower booking hall . . . I called to see if anybody was there, but could not hear any sound except the rushing water and hissing. It was gradually filling up. It was twenty feet in a gradual slope straight down the length of the station. The people were trapped directly beneath the slope, the heap of ballast near the emergency exit. The bomb had brought all the earth down on the inter-passage . . . I, the Divisional Traffic Inspector and two policemen decided to go back through the tunnel to Clapham South in case anyone was in the tunnels. It got deeper and deeper and we were pushing against the water . . .

We must hand it to the rescue people who came there. They did a wonderful job and started to bring out bodies between three and four in the morning. I had a horrible task to identify the bodies . . . There was the station master, a couple of porters, a booking clerk and his family . . .'

During the three months it took the police and emergency services to clear the debris, the bodies of some 64 shelterers and staff members were recovered. Bank, Sloane Square, Balham and Covent Garden were also to receive bomb damage during the war.

Policewoman at Waterloo, 1942.

Painting: Helen McKie, NRM/Science & Society Picture Library

As well as policing the railways, members of the LPTB were involved in detective duties for the London Aircraft Production Group, which produced more than 700 Halifax bombers, built bridging pontoons, assembled and tested lorries and over-hauled armoured vehicles; and for an aircraft components factory created in five miles of new and unused Central Line extension between Leytonstone and Gants Hill.

During the war Southampton was an important military port, designated a 'Protected Place' under the Defence Regulations. In the days preceding the invasion of Normandy work was intensified to an unprecedented level. And when the war was finally over, Docks Police had to oversee the to-ing and fro'-ing of thousands of British troops, overseas allies and prisoners of war.

Despite the employment of women and pensioners, by June 1941 the Railway Companies were struggling to retain sufficient numbers of officers. The staffing figures for all of the main line railway companies and the London Passenger Transport Board stood at:

Superintendents	24
Inspectors	147
Detective Sergeant	159
Uniform Sergeants	252
Detectives	320
Constables	2,961
Women police	34
Trainees and probationers	11
Total	3,908

In consequence, the Staff Committee suggested that Railway Police Forces should be scheduled by the Minister of Home Security as 'Civil Defence Forces' in order that recruitment of staff for the Railway Police Forces could be effected through the machinery of the National Service Act of 1941. Every man under 50 and every woman under 30 became liable for government assignment, producing 2,800,000 new war workers, 79% of which were female.

When the War finally ended in 1945, delight and relief were the order of the day. Normality gradually returned, but with the on-set of nationalisation, morale and loyalty were never to be the same again.

Courtesy of Science & Society Picture Library.

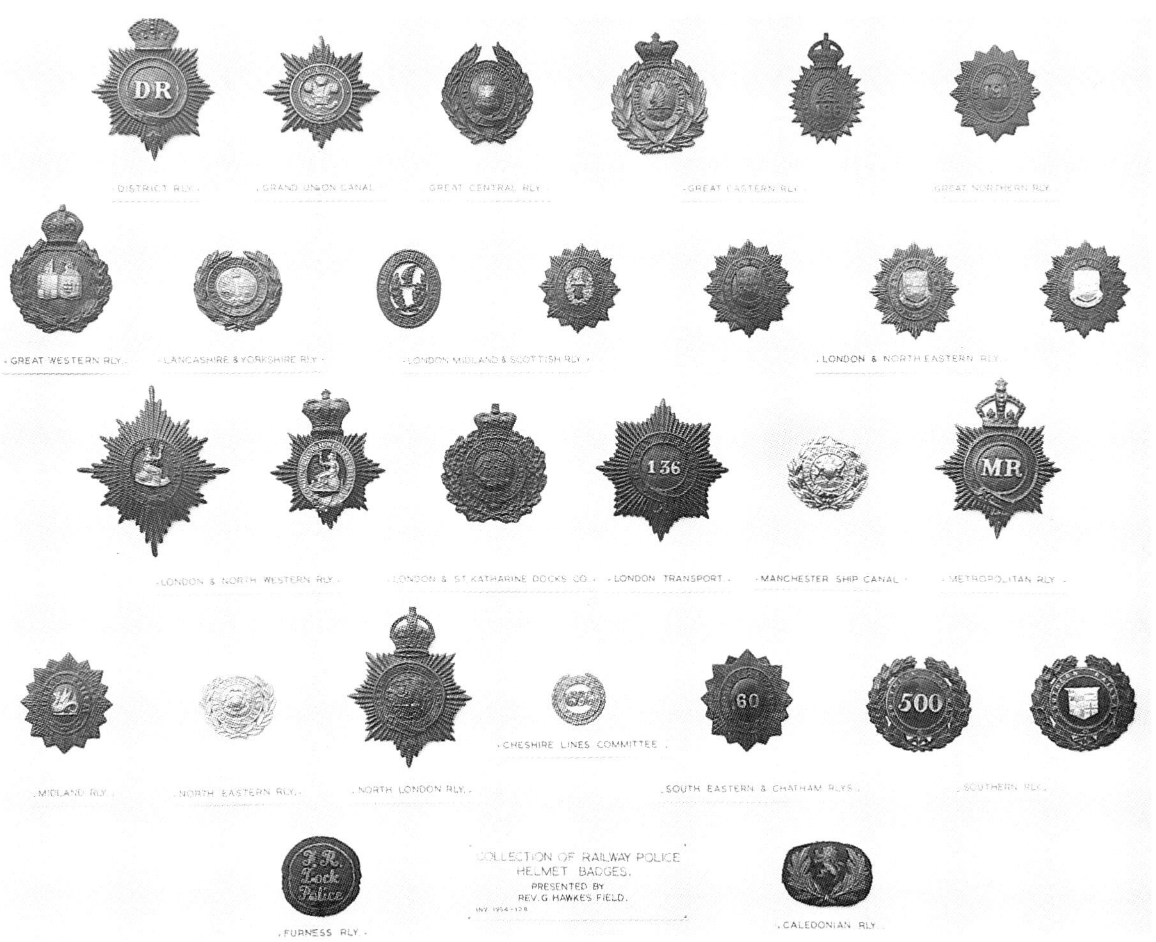

Chapter Six

NATIONALISATION

The enforced co-ordination of the railways had worked well under enormous pressures during the war years; and for some months afterwards the Railway Executive remained in control. The LPTB, for instance, continuing to look after London Buses (Green Line and London County), bus stands and depots; and to accompany paymasters in custom-built armoured vehicles over the London Transport area, ensuring that wages were safely delivered.

The Transport Act of 1947 was simply a natural progression that unified the railway systems of England, Scotland and Wales. Under the terms of the Act, control was handed back to the Railway Companies, the four group companies were abolished and in 1948 the British Transport Commission came into being, responsible for all railways and their undertakings, including ports, hotels, London Transport, inland waterways and long distance road haulage. In reality a number of Executives were created, responsible for various transport functions – including the London Transport Executive which retained its own police force of former LPTB officers.

Nationalisation divided the country into six regions: Scotland, North Eastern, Eastern, Southern, Western and London Midland. However, during 1948 officers remained operational within their previous railway regions, resulting in much unnecessary duplication of work. The Chiefs of Police remained in charge of their own departments: Mr A Lane for GWR, Mr W B 'Dickie' Richards for LMS, Colonel J Cole for Northern LMS and Colonel N Jesper for the Southern Area of LMS, and Mr W Growden for SR.

250 2/45

D 29

The London & North Eastern Railway Company

Justices' Certificate of Appointment

We, the undersigned, being two of His Majesty's Justices of the Peace having jurisdiction in the

__Borough__ of __Grimsby__

do hereby, upon the application of the London & North Eastern Railway Company, pursuant to the provisions of the London & North Eastern Railway Act, 1924, appoint

Arthur Hollingsworth

to act as a Constable in on and in the vicinity of the whole of the railways, stations, works and undertakings in England and Wales now or hereafter belonging or leased to or worked by the Company either solely or jointly with any other Company or Companies or to or by any Joint Committee now or hereafter incorporated or constituted by Act of Parliament on which the Company may be represented.

Given under our hand this __19th.__

day of __June,__ 19__46__

at the __Grimsby Borough__ Court.

__M. G. Smith__

Two of His Majesty's Justices of the Peace for

the said __Borough__ of __Grimsby.__

If lost, 2s. 6d. reward will be paid on its restoration to the Chief of Police, North Eastern Area, London and North Eastern Railway, York.

The feelings towards nationalisation were mixed; some officers were apprehensive but many hoped for a marked improvement in their role and status. Their hopes were encouraged by the appointment of the much loved Sir William 'Bill' Slim, Commander of the 14th Army in Burma who became Deputy Chairman of the Commission's Railway Executive. He had especially asked to take on the responsibility because he would 'feel at home among disciplined uniformed men and women'. He promised officers only his best, and told them that they now had someone at the top who was interested in them.

On 1st January 1949 Field Marshall Slim accepted a proposal to rectify the problem of work duplication and the British Transport Commission Police began to operate in the six areas:

Area	*Counties*	*Headquarters*	*Officers*
London	Metropolitan Police District and City of London	Euston Station	972
Scottish	Scotland	Glasgow	391
Northern	Cumberland, Westmoreland, Northumberland, Durham, Yorkshire	York	699
Midland	Lancashire, Cheshire, Staffordshire, Warwickshire, Oxfordshire, Worcestershire, Northamptonshire (part of), Herefordshire, Buckinghamshire (part of), Shropshire, North and Central Wales	Birmingham	786
Eastern	Derbyshire, Nottinghamshire, Lincolnshire, Buckinghamshire (part of), Northamptonshire (part of), Leicestershire, Rutland, Huntingdonshire, Hertfordshire, Bedfordshire, Cambridgeshire, Norfolk, Suffolk and Essex	Peterborough	445
South Western	Kent, Surrey, Sussex, Berkshire, Hampshire, Wiltshire, Gloucestershire, Monmouthshire, Glamorgan, Brecknock, Carmarthanshire, Pembrokeshire, Somerset, Dorset, Devon and Cornwall	Windsor	597

The London Transport Executive – not amalgamated with the British Transport Police until 1958 – was 100 officers strong, making a total of 3,990 officers. This total fell in 1956 to 3,006, with reductions in all areas, except London where the Transport Executive increased officer numbers by 12. The new Force was second in size only to the Metropolitan Police.

Answerable to the Chief Police Officer of the British Transport Commission was an Area Chief of Police, stationed at an Area Headquarters along with an Assistant Chief of Police, a Chief Clerk and a small civilian staff. A Chief Police Officer of the Commission, based at London Headquarters, co-ordinated the work of each Area, and communicated with the Commission through the Commission's Secretary General. The first to hold the post of Chief Police Officer in 1949 was Mr W B 'Dickie' Richards MVO, Chief of Police for the London Midland & Scottish Railway and a former LNWR man.

Sadly for the Force, in 1949 Bill Slim was recalled to the Army as Chief of the Imperial General Staff, Head of the British Army. He had made a significant mark on the Force, including obtaining the Crown to be worn on all police badges, and was very much respected by all.

Following the establishment of the six district areas, it was necessary to extend Railway Police powers to cover all the undertakings of the Commission. This was achieved by Section 53 of the British Transport Commission Act 1949, which reads:

'Subject to the conditions hereinafter set forth any two justices may on the application of the Commission appoint all or as many as they think fit of the persons recommended to them for that purpose by the Commission to act as Constables, in, on and in the vicinity of the whole of the railways, harbours, docks, inland waterways, stations, wharves, garages, hotels, works depots, and other premises in England and in Wales, now or hereafter belonging to, leased to, or worked by the Commission and the following provisions shall apply to every appointment so made:

(a) Every person so appointed shall make oath or declaration in due form of law before any justice having jurisdiction in any one of the counties, cities or boroughs in which such person is to act duly to execute the office of a Constable;

(b) Every person so appointed and having been sworn or having made declaration as aforesaid, shall during the continuance of his appointment have all the powers protection and privileges of a Constable in respect of the exercise of his duties, and may follow and arrest any person who has committed in, on or in the vicinity of, such railways, harbours, docks, inland waterways, stations, wharves, garages, hotels, works depots or other premises, any offence for which he might have been arrested while in, on or in the vicinity of the same;

Provided that no such powers shall be exercised outside the limits of the premises of the Commission except in regard to matters in connection with or affecting the Commission or their undertaking;

(c) Any two justices assembled and acting together or the Commission may dismiss from his office or accept the resignation of any Constable so appointed and thereupon all powers, protection and privileges belonging to such person by virtue of such appointment shall wholly cease. No person so dismissed or resigning shall be capable of being re-appointed except with the consent of the authority by whom he was dismissed or by whom his resignation was accepted;

(d) The police authority of any Area shall not be liable for any expense of, or be responsible for any acts or defaults of such Constables or for anything connected with, or consequent upon their appointment, and nothing in this act shall restrict or affect the jurisdiction or powers of any such police authority, or of any police force under their control;

(e) A person appointed as aforesaid shall not act as a

Constable under the authority of this Act, unless he be in uniform or provided with an authority to act as such, which authority the justice before whom such person makes oath or declaration as aforesaid is hereby empowered to grant, and if the Constable be not in uniform he shall use such authority whenever called upon to do so.'

In addition, the Force was awarded with powers to stop and search employees in the vicinity of a goods area.

The Oath of Office remained the same as that taken by Railway Constables since 1831, the only exception being that jurisdiction was now on a national basis and not limited to the undertaking of one particular railway company:

'I . . . do swear by Almighty God that I will, without favour or affection, malice or ill will, well and truly serve our Sovereign Lady, The Queen, in the Office of Constable in, on, and in the vicinity of all lands and premises of or under the control of the British Transport Commission in England and Wales, and that I will to the best of my power cause the peace to be kept and preserved, and prevent all offences against the persons and property of Her Majesty's subjects and that while I continue to hold the said office, I will to the best of my skill and knowledge discharge all duties thereof faithfully and according to the law. So help me God.'

October 1948 had also seen the first publication of the Railway (later British Transport) Police Journal. Sir Cyril Hurcomb GCB, KBE, Chairman of the British Transport Commission and General Sir William Slim, GBE, KCB, DSO, MC sent messages wishing it every success. It continued to be published until 1990 when it was replaced by the *Blue Line.*

Directing traffic at London's Kings Cross, 1950s.

An Inspector at Liverpool Lime Street. It was usual during the 1950s for officers in Lancashire and Liverpool Home Office forces to carry a nightstick. Liverpool division of BTCP also used the nightsticks for the purpose of banging the kerb to indicate to a beat constable where his presence was required.

Sealing and checking wagons during the 1950s.
Courtesy of Science & Society Picture Library

Following on from nationalisation, two Acts directly affecting the Force received Royal Assent in 1962. The first, the British Transport Commission Act, (1) provided for the issue of warrant cards signed by the Chief Constable, not Magistrates as had previously been the case; (2) stated that members of the Force were in future exempt from jury service; and (3) that the personation of a British Transport Commission police officer would be treated as an offence.

The second, the Transport Act, reconstituted the nationalised transport system of the country by the abolition of the British Transport Commission and the creation of five Boards: the British Railways Board, the London Transport Board, the Transport Holding Company, the British Transport Docks Board and the British Waterways Board. Section 60 also required a statutory scheme for the organisation of a unified transport police, thereby laying the foundations of the present Force: from 1st January 1963 the British Transport Commission Police would become, simply, the British Transport Police. The scheme contained provisions as to the:

1.   Control and administration of the Force by or on behalf of the Boards participating in the scheme by means of a British Transport Police Committee.

2.   Contributions to be made by those Boards to the expense of the Force.

3.   Method of settling disputes between those Boards and the Force.

The British Transport Commission Police (left) becomes the British Transport Police (right).

The Transport Act also provided for the Boards to establish a body comprising an equal number of representatives of the Board and non-managerial members of the Force, to which all questions relating to rates of pay, hours of duty and conditions of service would be referred. This allowed the British Transport Police Federation and the Superintendents' Association to be officially recognised as the negotiating body for all staff matters. Less popularly, the Act lost the Transport Police their pay parity with other forces, demoralising officers to the extent that many put in for transferrals.

Chapter Seven

TRAINING

The training of the early Railway Police was very basic – a few verbal instructions, the issue of a police manual and a few weeks on the beat with an experienced officer. As was the case with many police forces, with the notable exception of the Metropolitan Police, it was not until nationalisation after World War II that training became more formalised and comprehensive.

Before World War I the former North Eastern Railway, a constituent company of LNER, had provided facilities for education and mutual improvement of its police officers under Captain Horwood and, in the 1920s and '30s, began sending its recruits to the Metropolitan Training School at Peel House in London, founded in 1907 by Sir Edward Henry, or to a large county force. There were also some excellent detective training courses in various parts of the country, the most notable one being held at Scotland Yard, Headquarters of the Metropolitan Force since the mid-19th century.

With the recruitment drive that would be necessary following World War II, the subject of training had to be afforded appropriate consideration, and members of the Railway Executive decided to raise the proposal of a Railway Police training school at the Railway Staff Conference in December 1944. The proposal was accepted and officers from each Force were nominated to attend the Metropolitan Police Training Centre where preparations would be made, and a syllabus created. The officers were:

Assistant to Chief of Police	W O Gay	GWR
Assistant to Chief of Police	G Carvosso	GWR
Detective Inspector	E A Moody	LNER
Inspector (1st Class)	S P Small	LM & SR
Inspector (1st Class)	J A Clark	LNER
Inspector (2nd Class)	E C Hunt	LPTB
Inspector (3rd Class)	R Lancaster	LNER
D/Sergeant	A S Pooley	LNER
D/Sergeant	J O'Neil	LM & SR
D/Sergeant	F Brewer	SR
D/Sergeant	J R Stevens	SR
Sergeant	J R Hill	LM & SR
Sergeant	P A Longland	SR

During 1945 suitable premises were sought and three likely properties were located: Beenham Grange at Aldermaston, Berkshire; 'Newberries', an RAF property at Radlett, Hertfordshire; and St Cross, a former boys school in Walton on the Hill, Tadworth, Surrey.

'Newberries' was the first option but Middlesex County Council had made a previous offer and the Railway Executive settled for St Cross. The school was eventually purchased in July 1946 at a cost of £22,000, with the benefit of a claim for dilapidations against the War Department of up to £3,000.

The Chief of Police Conference then set up a training sub-committee who agreed that recruit courses would be of 13 weeks duration and that the school would be headed by a Commandant. Mr Frankton, former Commandant of the Metropolitan Police Training School was subsequently appointed – a controversial choice as some members felt strongly that the job should have gone to someone from a Railway Police force, such as Mr G Stephens, Chief of Police of the GWR. Mr Frankton was to be aided by a Deputy Commandant, Detective Sergeant Brewer of the Southern Railway, who set about preparing a Police Manual for use by all Railway Police Forces.

ST CROSS

St Cross School had been built in 1911 on the site of a small brick kiln, with ponds and scrubland adjoining the site of a Roman villa; and during World War II had been occupied by Canadian Armed Forces as a convalescent home. In 1945 the building had been requisitioned by the War Office Selection Board. On their departure the building required a great deal of repair and renovation and this was initiated as soon as the Railway Executive had made its purchase.

Main line Railways Police Training School, 1947.

Whilst repair work was being carried out, the instructors set up a classroom in rooms at Euston, left empty since the LMS office staff had evacuated to Watford during the hostilities. On the return of the LMS staff, the newly acquired offices had to be surrendered and classes

Tadworth today.

transferred to Tadworth, with students travelling to and from their homes daily or boarding in lodgings near-by. There were no canteen facilities available so attendees took their own refreshments and were taught amongst the dust and noise of the builders and decorators. Classes ran daily from 9.45 a.m. to 4.30 p.m., with equipment requisitioned from the Southern Railway, including tables and chairs, a tea urn and 50 copies of Moriarty's Police Law. Two cottages were requisitioned by the local authority for use as accommodation by the Commandant and his deputy in near-by Sandlands Grove.

Detective Inspector Moody (LNER) and Sergeant Hill (LMSR) were appointed as permanent instructors at the school, with other Forces to provide additional instructors on a rota basis. In addition, recruits were to receive training from experts in criminal investigation from the Metropolitan Police, and from other transport officials. Selected officers also attended specialist Home Office courses. In December 1947 Sergeant Laflin was appointed as resident Duty Officer and Drill Instructor, and was to remain in that post for many years.

The Railway Executive Committee at the opening of the British Railways Police College at Tadworth, December 1948.

Courtroom practice in the old chapel.

Unarmed combat training.

On 18th December 1948 the Commissioner of the City of London Police, Lieutenant Colonel Sir Hugh Turnball KCVO, KBE officially opened the school as a residential college and in January 1949 the first fully residential course took place. The school comprised two classrooms, a mock court room in the former chapel, five dormitories, two bathrooms and accommodation for instructors and domestic staff. By now 679 officers had already attended Tadworth for training and the Force had become the second largest in the country with over 4,000 officers. Earlier in the year the first women trainees had joined their ranks.

Various 'openings' duly followed. On 7th September 1958 converted dormitories at Withybed, a nearby house, were taken over for male students, and on 7th August 1559 the old school gymnasium was replaced by the Assembly Hall and officially opened by the Right Honourable Lord Rusholme, then Chairman of the Police Committee. The school library was opened on 19th August 1965 by Sir Stanley Raymond, Chairman of the British Railways Board.

First Aid Class.

Due to financial restraints and the possibility of redevelopment of the area, the school closed on 1st January 1968, following Recruit Course No 132. The Chief Constable took the passing out parade on 2nd November 1967 in the presence of all the former Commandants and Deputy Commandants. Mr Blackmore, the gardener, and Mr Holmes, the odd job man, remained at the school to maintain the buildings and grounds until its future was decided. An application to build 107 houses and garages on the site was put forward by George Wimpey &

Co, but was turned down by Banstead District Council as the site is part of the London Green-belt.

Training for new recruits was resumed in Home Office training schools, and specialised railway training and refresher courses were held at the Railway Committee's new school at New Lodge in Windsor Forest, purchased by the British Transport Commission in 1949.

A mansion built in 1858-9 on the site of the former home of Lord Raleigh, New Lodge had been a wedding present from American Joshua Bates to his daughter, on the occasion of her marriage to the Belgian Minister, His Excellency S Van der Mayer; their descendants continued to live there until 1920. During the Second World War the building had been requisitioned as the Headquarters of the Czech Relief Organisation.

New Lodge.

A recruitment poster
from the 1960s.

Redevelopment having fallen through, the Force was delighted to see the Training Division move back to Tadworth to re-commence residential courses in April 1971. It was officially re-opened on 21st July 1971 by the Chairman of the Police Committee Sir Frederick Hayday CBE, attended by a number of distinguished guests: the VIP contingent approached the building between a guard of honour provided by the two courses that were currently in residence. Basic recruit training remained at the Home Office training schools, with recruits attending Tadworth for such specialist courses as Criminal Investigations, Radio Communications and Crime Prevention. In later years these extended to include computer training, major incident training and victim support.

With more courses being run, greater, modernised living space was needed, and in 1981 a 42-bedroom accommodation block was built at a cost of £440,000. Opened by ·Mr J G Urquhart, the Chairman of the Police Committee, on 23rd October 1981, the block was named after Robert Kidd, the first Railway Policeman to be murdered in the course of duty. At the same time, two of the dormitories in the main building were converted into a library and television/video studio. Mr Urquhart returned in 1984 to open the new Dog Training School.

In 1991 a further accommodation/study block was opened and named in 1993 in memory of Keith Winter. Winter had joined the Force as a cadet in Hull in 1964, becoming a Constable in 1967. On 23rd October 1970 a British Road Services lorry carrying a propane gas tank attempted to enter St Andrews Dock in Hull via a subway. The tank valve caught the overhead railway bridge, allowing gas to escape, and in the explosion that followed PC Winter received severe burns, later to die in hospital. He was 22 and had been married only five months.

As well as bedrooms, the Winter Block features state of the art classrooms, each equipped with television/video equipment. During the alterations, the old chapel, which had housed the mock court room, was demolished.

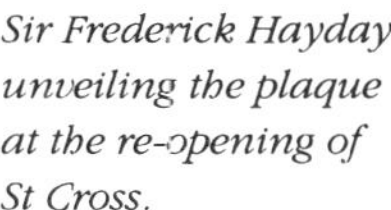

Sir Frederick Hayday unveiling the plaque at the re-opening of St Cross.

In 1994 'Speed Cuff' training replaced unarmed combat.

Preparing for PT.

Located close to the training school is Tadworth Court Trust, a hospital for physically and mentally handicapped children. Over the years staff and students have raised tens of thousands of pounds to support the home, the Force's name now added to the Trust's Major Benefactors Board. Tadworth also plays host to many meetings, conferences and events during the year, including the Force Dog Trials.

In the 50-odd years of the School's existence training has become highly comprehensive. Since the 1970s BTP recruits have been subject to the same entrance examination and training as their colleagues in Home Office forces. Today, they enter a two year probationary period, with training based around seven modules over a 32 week period, in accordance with Home Office policy, including one ten and one five week period at a Home Office Police Training Centre. In addition to teaching members of their own Force, BTP officers are occasionally seconded to the Senior Police Officers' Training College at Bramshill, the Central Planning and Training Unit at Harrogate, and Regional Crime Squad courses.

The 'Force Training Officer', based at Force Headquarters, has replaced the original 'Commandant', and 'Chief Inspector (Training)', based at Tadworth, replaces 'Deputy Commandant'. The school also has an administrative and domestic staff. In 1994 Mrs Sylvia Jobson, the House Manager and an integral and much loved figure within the school, was awarded an MBE for her services to the Force.

Chief Constable Desmond O'Brien and Mrs Sylvia Jobson, accompanied by Mrs O'Brien and Mrs Jobson's son, receiving honours.

CADET TRAINING

Between the end of the Second World War and the late 1950s, the Force was comprised of predominantly ex-military, older men, and a need for younger officers was identified. The introduction of cadet training, though costly, provided the answer, and in 1958 the Force began offering one course per year for boys aged between 16 and 19. These boys, who often still lived at home with their parents and had little previous exposure to the world at large, saw cadetship as an exciting challenge. After a six-week course at Tadworth they would be attached to an operational division to work with experienced officers and accompany them on their beats. They had no powers to investigate crime, carry handcuffs or truncheons, but they did gain essential experience of the specialised environment, the travelling public and the transport industry.

Chief Inspector Keith Groves became a cadet in 1969, attached to the Divisional Headquarters in Birmingham, and his experience was typical of many. After a course at Tadworth learning the basics of law and fitness, his cadetship involved him in clerical work at Divisional Headquarters and attachments to the Criminal Investigation Department. He also spent a four-week Outward Bound course at Erin Valley in mid-Wales, owned by the City of Birmingham Police. Groves shared a tent with seven other lads, and every morning they would have to present their kit for inspection, laying out their bedroll and even sweeping the grass it lay upon into neat lines. The course included a number of hikes, cook-house duties and finished up with the obligatory concert.

Elan Valley – Birmingham City Cadet Camp, 1968.

Inspector Brian Gosdon also joined the Force through a cadetship, attached to the Portsmouth Division in 1969, where all but one of the officers were aged between 50 and 55. He recalls how they treated him like a son, even taking him home for tea on the evenings of his first-aid class so that they could ensure he reached it on time. It was from these men that Brian learnt the art of good policing: not only to be firm with people who crossed their paths, but also to show compassion towards them.

Accompanied by WPC Betty Binns, Cadet Fred Whitfield gets a feel for working on the docks, Southampton 1966.

Cadets standing to attention for inspection, 1967.

In 1971 cadet training was reviewed by a committee and a more formal structure came into place. The objective was to 'produce young men of courage, character and intelligence with the physical requirements for entry into the Force'. 'Young men' became 'young men and women' in 1974 when female cadets were encouraged to apply. The new cadetship also lasted three years but was divided into three phases:

1.   Further Education.
2.   Discipline, mind broadening and character building.
3.   Equipping the cadet for the Police Force.

At the age of 16 the cadet would be sent to his local college of further education to study English Language, English Literature, Sociology, British Constitution, Law and Typing. Whilst the college was closed for the holidays, the cadet returned to his local division.

Between 17 and 18 years of age, the cadet attended an eight-week course at Tadworth, where 'discipline, mind broadening and character building' were achieved by lectures, organised visits and a week's expedition to Dartmoor. They were then seconded to their area British Rail Training Officer, British Transport Hotels Training Officer and Shipping and International Services Training Officer for a total period of nine weeks. For further experience, cadets were seconded for four-weekly periods to the Princess Marina Spastic Centre, British Rail Convalescent Home and the Southern Railwaymen's Home for Children, where they worked as members of staff. In this phase cadets also became members of the Conservation Corps, and received instruction in the preservation and improvement of the countryside in general. Further character building schemes involved cadets in a three-week Outward Bound Course at the West Yorkshire Outdoor Activity Centre.

In the final phase, cadets had the opportunity to attend the West Highland School of Adventure, Applecross, Scotland. They were also sent for four-weekly periods to the British Rail Scientific and Research Department, Force Headquarters and, for an appreciation of dock working, either to Southampton or to Hull Docks. Finally, they returned to Tadworth for a four-week recruit preparation course.

By the time they were 19, and eligible to join the Force as recruits, cadets were already several steps ahead of their peers. They would be sworn in as officers, take part in nine weeks of recruit training, and then be sent to a station for further on-the-job experience.

Cadet training was abolished in 1975 when the joint effects of the entry age to the Force being lowered from 19 to 18½ and rising unemployment improved recruitment prospects.

TULLIALLEN

The scattered population in Scotland means that policing has always been very community based, with excellent working relationships developing between BTP and the Home Office Forces. Prior to 1968 recruits were trained at Tadworth and at Strathclyde Police Training Center in Ayre; but in recent years links have been forged closer by the fact that BTP officers now attend the Scottish Police Training College at Tulliallen Castle, Kincardine, Alloa, alongside their local police counterparts. In addition, several Assistant Chief Constables (Scotland) have joined BTP from other Scottish Forces. Tulliallan is a

Passing out parade of recruits and cadets on 21st August, 1961, in presence of Mr K Gland, member of the Royal Transport Commission and Chairman of the Commission's Police Committee.

unique college, not only due to its location being inside a 'working' castle and surrounded by beautiful grounds, but also because all ranks of police officers are trained there, from new recruits to Chief Inspectors. Hanging in the porch is a lamp that was originally used on Lynedogh Station of the Glasgow & South Western Railway in 1869, and donated to the college 100 years later by the British Transport Police.

Tulliallan Castle

Chapter Eight

WOMEN IN THE FORCE

'. . . In 1914 Margaret Damer Dawson, together with her friend Miss Nina Boyle, began to enrol members for the Women's Police Volunteers. Public opinion raged; letters poured in to the press from the British Public who were "amazed at British women doing such grotesque things", but Margaret and Nina, undaunted, did such good work that the whole world, particularly the USA, began to sit up and take notice.'

Joyce Marsh, BTP Journal of April 1953

Whilst the employment of women police officers was to generate a variety of emotions for years to come, few people could question the growing need for it. During World War I nine women were sworn in as Special Constables on the LNER to replace officers serving overseas; they were followed by others at Marylebone, London, and York; and in the Second World War, with literally millions of men mobilised for military duty, more still. By 1942 numbers of women officers stood at:

London & North Eastern Railway	28
Great Western Railway	3
London Passenger Transport Board	5
Southern Railway	8

The end of the Second World War brought about massive change for the role of women in society. All over the country they had taken jobs in services and industries that had hitherto been purely male domain, and had proved that they could perform many tasks as well, and indeed some better, than their male counterparts. Prior to the War there were few acceptable jobs for a woman outside the home, the most notable being nurse or schoolteacher – and these were generally treated as a 'stop gap' until she had found a husband. But realisation was beginning to dawn that there were far more ways for a woman to fulfil her potential.

With the country plunged into massive economic chaos following the War, it was sometimes easier to retain the services of women in the workplace – for one thing they could be paid less – and inevitably the new level of independence women were gaining, was greeted with resentment and trepidation by the men returning home: they resented the fact that having fought for their country, they were effectively being rewarded by unemployment; and they feared for the future of their homes and families.

The various police forces were no exception with regard to the employment of women. At a meeting held at Euston Station on 26th February 1946, Chiefs of Police talked of the changing post-war attitudes and concerns, namely that women had proved themselves invaluable members of the Force performing a variety of duties. Whilst men had now returned, the meeting concluded that a quota of women 'in the establishment of each force' was desirable for dealing with incidents involving women and children.

Colonel Jesper of the LNER stated a recommendation that such women officers, when not actually engaged in police duties, could always be usefully employed on routine clerical duties at the divisional offices. The Chairman did point out that this might give rise to objections from the Railway Clerk's Association, hitherto employed for such duties, but the true concept of 'equal opportunities' was something that would not be at the forefront of their minds for some 40 years yet.

And so, a Women's Police Unit was created, with its own constitution within the Force. In the BTP Journal of 1973, Sergeant Smith described her duties at the port of Dover. These were 9 a.m. to 5 p.m . . .

> '. . . assisting with Boat Traffic, ensuring that all passengers passed through the Immigration and Customs Controls and looking after refused aliens . . . It soon became apparent to the supervisory officers that I could type . . . So I began to learn about ticket frauds by typing out statements and preparing papers for prosecution.'

Gradually Sergeant Smith's duties extended to cover all enquiry work concerning female offenders and witnesses throughout the Dover sub-division, which included the whole of Kent and a small part of Sussex. Occasionally she was also called upon to escort female 'aliens' over the Channel.

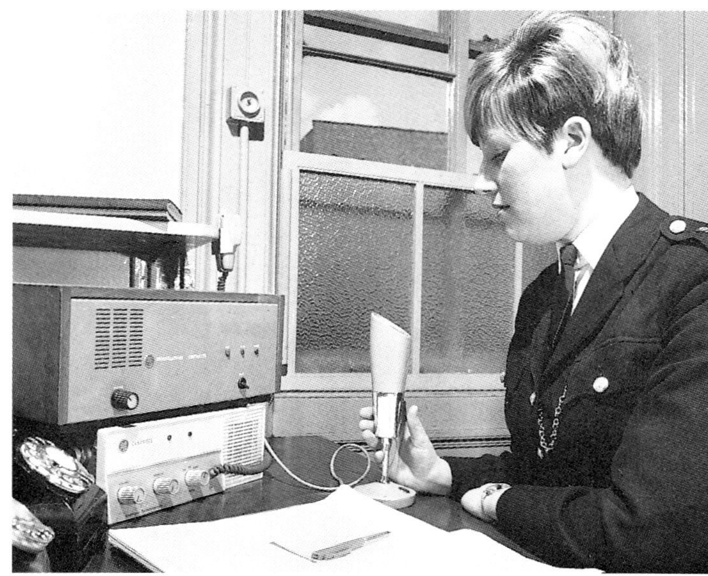

In the early days the policewoman's work was often limited to radio and clerical duties.

*Early 1960s.
Policewomen were
particularly
assigned to work
involving women
and children.*

*An inspection of
Policewomen on
Parade.*

In March 1961 Vera Lee, originally from North Riding Constabulary, was appointed the first Inspector on the Women's Unit, and in 1963 was promoted to the rank of Chief Inspector. Her appointment was a major breakthrough, although opportunities for women were still slow in coming about.

*Chief Inspector
Vera lee.*

*Winners of the
Grace Lucas Cup, 1963.*

Policewomen of the Manchester Division displaying their latest uniform, 1969.

When Margaret Lyall joined the Scotland Division she was typical of those women frustrated by the limitations imposed on her sex: they did not work on Sundays; they did not work night duties; they did not carry a baton; they dealt almost exclusively with women and children; and they were paid 10% less than men. However, pressures were building not just in the police forces, but in other services, too; and the 1970s saw a number of Acts passed: the Equal Pay Act of 1970, the Employment Act of 1972, the Fair Employment Act of 1974, the Sex Discrimination Act of 1975 and the Race Relations Act of 1976. In 1974 the Force encouraged the recruitment of women with a pilot scheme for women cadets, and with volume of numbers beginning to tip the balance, nightshifts were at last offered, although initially only to involve ticket enquiries and telephone duties. In the late 1970s, Margaret was licensed to drive police vehicles and, in the guise of an official driver, was finally able to work alongside her male colleagues. The uniform skirt was totally impractical for such activities as climbing into railway yards and Margaret managed to obtain a pair of men's uniform trousers from the Force tailor. When confronted, the logic of her attire was indisputable and today, policewomen can choose between skirts or trousers.

As the Women's Police Unit became a thing of the past, Joan Pilgrim was the first woman to be appointed Chief Inspector of the integrated Force. And in 1991 Chief Inspector Betty Glover became the first woman in charge of the Training School at Tadworth. She is now Officer In Charge at London's Waterloo, covering a total of 80 stations.

In 1995 policewomen perform exactly the same duties and receive the same pay as their male counterparts. They represent around 10% of the work force.

Patrolling close to Birmingham's famous Bull Ring Shopping Centre.

There for everyone . . .

POLICE DOGS

Ready for action!

THE HOUNDS FROM HULL

> 'These Railway Cops don't give you a dog's chance. As for
> the dogs, they look at you as though you were a tin o'
> Lassie.'

So commented a thief after being convicted of stealing coal from a
railway stock pile in 1958. He had been caught red-handed by police
dog 'Caro'.

Belgian Police at Ghent had been taking dogs with them on dock
patrol for some time before news of them reached Hull in the early
20th century. Their heightened sense of smell – the 'olfactory system' –
could root out contraband long before a human, and their sharp teeth
were an obvious deterrent for trespassers and those who, having been
caught, might consider taking off again. Railway Police Officers were
subsequently sent over to Belgium to study the role and training
methods of dogs, and their visit resulted in a number of Airedales
being introduced to police duty at Hull Docks in 1908. Various breeds
were tested for suitability, but the Airedale, with its stocky build,
courageous spirit and sound temperament, remained firm favourite
until the 1920s when the German Shepherd was found to be faster,
more agile and generally more versatile than the Airedale. Its wolfish
looks demand great respect from the general public and the thickness
and coarseness of its coat means that it can stand Britain's coldest
weather.

Dogs were an immediate success. Beat officers were full of praise
for their canine colleagues, although dockside thieves were not so
impressed. An article entitled 'Dog Detectives' in the *Penny Pictorial* of
25th June 1910 described their work in some detail:

> 'The force of Police dogs at Hull consists of a number of
> trained Airedale Terriers, which, in the company of the
> Railway Police, patrol the Hull docks throughout the night
> and capture thieves, tramps and any other persons who may

be sleeping out. Each dog has to undergo a special and most elaborate training and the first thing he is taught is that every person not dressed in Police uniform is an enemy. The dogs are trained to obey a Police whistle, and then to chase and stop a man who is running away, and hold him till the officer arrives.'

North Eastern Railway Police Sergeant Allison with 'Jim' at Hull Docks, c. 1910.

Such was the Hull dogs' reputation that during the First World War, the Royal Northumberland Fusiliers took a number of them to France where they were used to retrieve and carry messages through the trenches. Trained by Colonel Richardson, the dogs performed sterling service, for the most part undeterred by the gunfire and shelling taking place around them.

In 1913 'Charlie', of Hull & Barnsley Railway Police, was the first police dog to be honoured with a shield and silver medal of the Canine Heroes League. He won the award for saving his handler's life when a foreign seaman attacked him with a knife. The award was followed by a Certificate of Merit at Crufts Dog Show.

Constable Easton and Charlie.

The idea of dogs aiding in police work took some time to be accepted by the general public. One old lady who spotted tracker dogs at work, is known to have remarked: 'Fancy hunting the poor man with those dogs, it's dreadful and in-human.' She was duly informed that the 'poor man' was being pursued for beating and severely injuring a similar old lady to herself.

During the Second World War, when so many docks officers were serving overseas, the use of dogs was minimal; but with kennels situated on the docks themselves, the dogs did not miss out on the action. During one incident the kennels on Hull's Albert Dock were blasted by High Explosive, and several dogs escaped into the smoking ruins of the much battered city. Some were rounded up, some returned to the site of their kennel of their own accord, but one 'enterprising and sagacious animal' was found on Paragon Station attempting to board a train bound for Brough in the Yorkshire Wolds. Apparently he had had enough of city life and decided to join the ever growing army of evacuees.

Courtesy of the NRM/
Science and Society Picture Library

With the return to normality after the War, dogs became more popular for police work, and the Force began experimenting with a breeding programme as well as buying in new stock. In 1958 Dorothy Campion, author of *The Perfect Team*, frequently referred to the dogs being unmuzzled – unusual at the time but demonstrating the level of discipline at which they could work. Of the British Transport Commission dogs she remarked:

> 'In a way these dogs have a tougher battle against crime to fight than the City Police Dog. The BTC dog and handler work a lone beat and help cannot be called for. These men have terrific faith and confidence in their dogs.'

An NER policeman and dog at Hull Docks, 1950.

By 1951 police dogs were well established in the North Eastern area and were becoming more familiar in other parts of the country. In the 1951 Journal Sergeant R Galway wrote of a demonstration of Hull dogs that would 'leave no doubt whatsoever of its capabilities and the value of its usage when correctly utilised.' Subsequent demonstrations and shows did indeed result in Hull dogs attaining celebrity status, with a waiting list for further appearances. The dogs enjoyed these outings and their high profile almost certainly acted as a deterrent to would-be dock thieves.

Gushetfaulds Freightliner Terminal, Glasgow, 1966.

HEDON

In the early 1950s a convalescent home for horses at Hedon near Hull, was requisitioned for the training of dogs under Inspector Morrell. There was no official course structure and police officers were given just two days to learn how to handle their new dog. German Shepherd dogs were now used exclusively, and were accepted for training between one and two years of age.

In 1962 running of the school was taken over by Inspector, later Chief Inspector, Herbert (Terry) Shelton. Shelton had joined the Metropolitan Police Dog Section in 1946 as one of six handlers who were part of a Home Office experiment to measure the effectiveness of dogs as an aid to policing. He had subsequently helped to establish a dog training school within the Metropolitan Police Force, along with Superintendent Stanley Peck who eventually became a member of the HM Inspector of Constabulary, and had travelled extensively to promote the use of dogs in other forces. By the time Shelton arrived at Hedon, some 30 dogs were being employed at different locations around the country, kennelled at such central points as old stables in sidings and goods yards. With the Transport Police in the middle of extensive reorganisation following the Maxwell-Johnson Enquiry, police dogs became the responsibility of Area Assistant Chief Constables.

Upon arrival Shelton set about giving the section some structure. He planned a detailed ten-week training programme, including lectures on canine health and grooming, and arranged for the building of kennels-and-runs at handlers' homes so that following the training period handlers and dogs could maintain the closeness necessary for an effective working partnership. Seventy-five dogs were to be trained to operate nationally, and courses were soon being run consecutively. Handlers finished with a clear understanding of how to continue day-to-day training upon their return to the station, with refresher courses and continuation training arranged for two weeks of every year. From the 1960s onwards, all dogs were obtained from private homes rather than bred by the Force, as 'socialisation' was now recognised as essential in the development of a balanced temperament – dogs that had been living in a family household for the early months of their lives were far more able to cope with everyday situations than those raised in breeding kennels.

In 1963 Hedon hosted the first Annual Working Trials for British Transport Police dog handlers. These aimed to judge, by practical tests, the standard achieved by the dog and handler as a team. Each Area Commander would select two dogs and their handlers to compete for the John William Morrell Trophy (donated by Mrs Winifred Morrell, widow of the late Inspector John Morrell), the Big Ben Trophy (donated by Chief Inspector Shelton) and the Diligence Trophy.

As more novice dogs and handlers joined the Force every year, so the number of teams returning to Hedon for refresher courses swelled. Dogs were also returned for boarding if their handler was sick or on annual leave and, of course, new dogs had to be housed whilst they were assessed for suitability. By 1965 the school at Hedon had out-grown itself and new premises were sought in which to extend training facilities. Plans were drawn up and a suitable location found at Elstree in Hertfordshire. The new training school was staffed by Chief Inspector Shelton, and Sergeant Len Austin, who had previously been employed at Kings Cross Station, where he looked after the kennelled dogs.

The training centre at Elstree.

Part of the new curriculum for trainee handlers was to feed, groom and exercise their dogs prior to the day's training. Most of the training was carried out at the school, but tracking and Area Search practice took place in surrounding locations, for which purpose a large van was purchased and fitted out with six cages and six seats – for dogs and officers respectively! A probationary period was spent with novice dogs and handlers getting to know each other and developing a bond; then the real training began, progressing through increasingly difficult stages, with handlers taught to coax the best out of their dogs using patience, firmness and understanding.

During the years that followed the establishment of the new training centre police dogs became increasingly effective; but in 1975 Chief Constable Haslam decided the school was economically inviable and it was closed. Around 70 dogs were in service, of which 50 were put to early retirement. The Crewe division of the BTP were amongst those lucky enough to retain a couple of dogs for police work, and between January and March of 1978 'Nikki' and 'Rick' assisted in 13 arrests, 42 detections, and 12 incidents of football hooliganism.

Police dog 'arresting' a criminal.

Chief Inspector Shelton also retired. Affectionately remembered for his 'hands like shovels', he had been highly respected and admired by all those who worked with him. In the following years refresher courses and basic training continued on a very small scale at Home Office dog training schools; but the closure was seen by many as a false economy which had left the remaining dog handlers with no direct leadership.

In the early 1980s Ginge Ablard was promoted to Sergeant, overseeing the dog section of which he had been a part since 1969, and a sense of direction began to re-emerge (he was later awarded a BEM for his work). Following requests from Mr Stanley Peck, now a member of the Police Committee, and Chief Superintendent George Smith-Leach, later to become Assistant Chief Constable (Scotland), the appointment of a Dog Training Inspector was approved – John Lloyd, who had been on active service with the Metropolitan Police Dog Section – along with the reintroduction of a BTP dog training school.

In 1983 the purpose built school was established at Tadworth, and Inspector Lloyd effected a new training programme entailing a 12-week basic course, an annual three-week refresher course and monthly continuation training. He also reinstated the Annual Working Trials, in which ten handlers are selected to compete in obedience, agility, tracking, and search tests.

SPECIALIST SEARCH DOGS

On the Force today there are two types of police dog. German Shepherds are used as 'Patrol Dogs' for the front line detection and prevention of crime, and at incidents of public disorder; whilst Labradors or Springer Spaniels, introduced in 1981, are used as 'Specialist Search Dogs'.

Specialist Search Dogs receive their basic training at designated Home Office training centres over an eight-week period where, in addition to dog handling, owners learn about different types of explosives and their accompanying devices.

Dog teams are the first to search potential bomb areas, for example VIP and Royal Trains, Political Party Conferences and nuclear flask movements. They work in pairs, one team searching, the other acting as a 'spotter' of hazards. Once a bomb has been located, the teams fall back to allow specialist bomb disposal officers to take over. An enormous amount of travelling is required to provide a nation-wide service, with British Transport and Home Office Forces lending each other support where necessary.

PC John Warner and PC 'Slim' Townsend, Euston, 1973.

THE LOCKERBIE AIR DISASTER

In the Scottish Division, all handlers work both types of dog – requiring extensive training, skill and experience. The tragedy that occurred on 21st December 1989 in the small town of Lockerbie was to test those skills to the full. During the course of the Boeing 747 explosion – the alleged work of Libyan terrorists – the 259 passengers, crew, luggage and airliner were strewn over 54 square miles, the centre fuselage and wings crashing down on a residential area and destroying some 20 houses. Within an hour of the explosion, PCs Davey Connell and Alistair Campbell had arrived with their dogs to begin a gruelling 33-hour shift, during which time they discovered the bodies of 23 passengers. PCs Callum Weir and Neil Russell joined the search on the second day, and all four remained until the end of the operation four weeks later. Home Office Forces and dogs, Search and Rescue Dogs from the local mountain rescue teams, and representatives from Boeing, Pan Am and the Air Accident Investigation Branch also joined in. Gruelling weather conditions, the continual presence of press people and onlookers, and the knowledge that Christmas was traditionally a joyous celebration, combined to make this a difficult time for everyone concerned; but strong bonds were to develop between the teams, who received commendations for their work, and not surprisingly there followed a long period of readjustment to normal routine.

Although there is no sex discrimination in the appointment of dog handlers, very few women have opted to take the role. Margaret Lyall was the first woman dog handler, training with her dog 'Denny' at Strathclyde in Glasgow in 1983. After qualifying they were based in Glasgow and the West of Scotland for a number of years; but a shoulder injury later necessitated that Margaret transfer to another specialist branch and Denny was retired early. As is usual, Denny was allowed to remain with Margaret as a pet. In 1995 PC Judy Bailey, a Specialist Search Dog handler, remains the only woman in the dog section.

Investigating an incident at sidings in Birmingham.

Chapter Ten

THE MAXWELL -JOHNSON ENQUIRY

Since its inception the British Transport Commission had consistently set pay levels lower than the Home Office. Independent arbitrators were frequently engaged to negotiate a settlement, and in May 1956 Mr H Lloyd Williams at last awarded pay parity, although with no allowances. Overnight, what was seen as an already expensive Force had become even more costly. As a result, the following year the British Transport Commission initiated an enquiry into the most efficient way of policing its undertakings.

The Government appointment of two eminent authorities, Sir Alexander Maxwell CBE and Mr W C Johnson CMG, CBE, was regarded as a great compliment to the BTCP. Since retiring from his position of Permanent Under Secretary of State at the Home Office in 1948, a position he had held for ten years, Sir Alexander Maxwell had conducted many key enquiries on behalf of the Government. Mr Johnson had led an equally distinguished career. Following service in the Royal Engineers during the First World War, he had joined the police service at Portsmouth. In 1932, when Superintendent of CID, he had been promoted to Chief Constable of Plymouth. He moved on to Birmingham in 1936, initially as Assistant Chief Constable and then as Chief Constable, finally becoming one of Her Majesty's Inspectors – Inspector General of the Colonial Police – and visiting many Commonwealth countries in that capacity.

Sir Alexander Maxwell.

Mr Johnson.

Aided by the Assistant to the Chief Legal Advisor of the Commission, Mr G S M Birch TD, Sir Alexander and Mr Johnson toured the country from top to bottom, interviewing officers of all ranks. Their conclusions were unanimous: that the maintenance of a British Transport Police Force was essential to the country's transport system. Their subsequent recommendations, aimed at improving the Force's administration and command, included the appointment of a Chief Constable and a Police Committee. Mr Arthur West was duly appointed Chief Constable and Lord Rusholme appointed Chairman of the Police Committee. West had come to the Force from Hampshire, where he was Chief Constable of Portsmouth during the Second World War. His influence on the Force included a reorganisation of the CID departments, which restricted CID duties to the investigation of crime, and the appointment of a Chief of Police (Crime) to be based at new headquarters in Park Royal, North West London.

Park Royal.

The recommendations of the Maxwell Johnson Enquiry were:

1. To maintain a unified force, organised and trained and equipped so as to provide an efficient police service, for all the varied undertakings of the Commission.

2. To re-align the various police areas, with changes of Area Headquarters.

3.   The merging of London Transport Police into the main body of the Force, as a special division.

4.   To re-organise the Criminal Investigation Department of the Force, and to establish a Criminal Records Office.

5.   The Chief Constable to undertake, in consultation with the appropriate departments of the Commission and subject to the views of the Police Committee, a review of the establishment of the Force.

6.   To expand the training facilities for recruits and senior officers at the Commission's Police School, and to increase the number of officers attending specialised CID courses at Home Department detective training centres.

7.   To initiate a scheme for the adequate training of police cadets.

8.   To introduce an appropriate method of dealing with alleged disciplinary offences by members of the Force.

By and large these recommendations were effected, beginning in 1958 with the amalgamation of the London Transport Police into the British Transport Police. One hundred and thirteen police officers, eight clerks and two testers joined BTCP, with Chief Inspector Alfred Peedle appointed Superintendent In Charge who reported, in turn, to Chief Constable Arthur West.

The opening of the new Headquarters at Park Royal on 15th October 1959 was a major turning point. For the first time, a properly-suited central office could control and supervise the growing Force. Within HQ, a Criminal Records Office was set up, with specialist CID teams investigating crimes on a national level. Recruit training was extended at Tadworth, and Home Office CID training maximised.

Scottish BTP officers wear a diced hat band, similar to that of Scottish Home Office Forces.

A further turning point was the creation of a 94-strength Warden Security Corps in 1960. Wardens were authorised to take over such duties as general security of goods entering or leaving the Commission's premises, and locking railway wagons and road vehicles, thereby relieving police officers for more active work. The Chief Constable was responsible for their administration, and the police department responsible for expenditure.

In line with Sir Alexander Maxwell's recommendation, a further enquiry was conducted in 1961, this time by Sir Frank Newsam, formerly of the Department of Transport. The objectives were:

1. To determine the establishment of the Force.

2. To consider particular duties of officers such as the control of entrances to goods depots.

3. To examine the ratio of uniformed officers to CID and that of supervisory officers in each branch.

4. To examine the question of retaining police officers at 'one-man' posts.

5.   To work out a plan for improving the promotion prospects of policewomen.

6.   To consider the extended use of police dogs.

Some of Newsam's findings and subsequent recommendations were to prove controversial and unpopular with members of the Force. For a start, he proposed the reduction of 513 officers nationally – arising from a theory that the correct formula for police establishment should be based on a ratio of officers to railway employees. He further recommended that railway and police management should agree upon an order of priority for police services, and that more time should be spent on the investigation of serious offences. Significantly, no mention was made of the public interest.

He proposed the abolition of one-man posts as they were uneconomic; and claimed officers would be more effective in dealing with thefts on stations if they were deployed in plain clothes. The investigation of ticket offences was also identified as using a disproportionate expenditure of police time, and a more efficient procedure was to be formulated.

Of the London Transport Police Division, however, Newsam's review stated:

> ' . . . we have no hesitation in reaching the conclusion that this unit of the Commission's Force is well organised and efficiently operated to provide specialised services required by the Executive with whom there exists the fullest measure of liaison and collaboration.'

The Division was forthwith upgraded to an 'Area', with the Superintendent becoming the Area Chief, later Commander or Assistant Chief Constable, and the Chief Inspector becoming Superintendent. Divisional Headquarters at this time were situated in Broadway, with sub-divisions at Baker Street and Lambeth North. Each sub-division was responsible for the full range of police work, including uniform patrol and criminal investigations. By the 1970s the Area was 140-officers strong, and covered a 25 mile radius around Charing Cross, containing 120 bus depots and garages, 231 railway stations and 223 miles of railway, over which 2,601 million passenger journeys were made every year. By the mid-1990s the London Underground Area had grown to encompass 278 stations and surrounding premises, with around 800 million passenger journeys being made each year, policed by an establishment of 425 officers and supported by around 60 civilian staff.

A Constable assists young train-spotters at Kings Cross, 1963.

PC Deacon at Borough Station, 1975.

Among Newsam's proposals had been the suggestion that additional civilian support staff should be employed to release officers for police duties. The Warden Security Corps scheme was declared false economy, and the duties fell first to the control of railway traffic managers, but then, eventually, back to police officers.

A policewoman at Glasgow Central Station in 1963, soon after the disbanding of the BT Commission, wearing the new Force cap badge.

The British Transport Police Force Scheme was laid before Parliament in September 1964, and came into operation on 1st January 1965. It provided for the Force to be organised into Divisions, with a chief officer officially entitled Chief Constable.

In 1963 Arthur West retired from the Force. His successor as Chief Constable was William Owen Gay, who had joined the Great Western Railway Police after leaving university and had steadily worked his way up to the rank of Chief of Police (Crime). He was a prolific writer on Police and Law subjects, and regularly contributed to the British Transport Police Journal and Police Review. O Gay decided that his first task must be to set about improving morale within the Force, chiefly by restoring pay parity with Home Office Forces. He achieved this by producing evidence to show that financial constraints were pushing so many trained men over to Home Office Forces, the disparity could only be considered false economy. Pay was accordingly raised, along with a supplementary allowance to be paid in lieu of the rent allowance paid to civil police. In addition, a Special Police Pension Scheme was brought in, payable at the age of 55 and subject to the completion of 30 years service, which enabled officers to retire younger, thereby lowering the average age in the Force.

William O Gay.

In 1972 Mr S Lawrence CBE, QPM, a former member of the HM Inspector of Constabulary and member of the British Transport Police Committee, was invited to further investigate and report on the work, organisation and size of the Force. Mr Lawrence produced two reports, one relating to London Transport and one to British Rail.

For London Transport, he recommended an increase in manpower, better radio communications, improved reporting methods and more civilian staff. He also drew attention to the increasing crime rate and incidents of football hooliganism. For the British Rail Board, he recommended an increase of 150 police officers, more clerical staff, and improved communications.

Mr Eric Haslam, former Deputy Chief Constable of the Kent Constabulary, took over from William O Gay on his retirement in 1975. Under Mr Haslam's direction, a number of dramatic changes took place: the dog training school was closed, cadet training ceased and, rather more popularly, the introduction in 1979 of the Police Information System (PINS). Through PINS, BTP became the first Force to record crime reports using a computer. Together with a network of nation-wide communications, the System now allows officers anywhere in the country to access information held on a continually updated data base.

During 1978 the Right Honourable Lord Edmund-Davies chaired a Committee of Enquiry to review the procedure by which pay and conditions of police service were negotiated. The resulting report recommended substantial pay increases for Home Office Forces, again leaving BTP officers behind. Morale dropped to an all-time low, and applications for transfer began to pour in. A further enquiry was initiated into the pay and conditions for non-Home Office Forces, chaired this time by E D Wright CB. The combined work of the British Transport Police Federation and Mr Basil Nichols, Assistant Chief Constable (Operations), resulted in a committee recommendation that British Transport Police should become the only non-Home Office Force to achieve 100% pay parity.

A further inspection of the Force was carried out in December 1979 by R S Barratt, HM Inspector of Constabularies. He concluded that the Force was under-manned which, by definition, created some distance between police locations, increasing problems of supervision and reinforcement of officers in emergencies. He pinpointed two other difficulties unique to the British Transport Police:

1. They were operating within commercial constraints (common-place to all forces by the 1990s).

2. They were operating with the varying policies of some 50 local forces and many more Magistrates court areas.

Mr Kenneth Ogram, formerly of Leeds City Police, took over the post of Chief Constable in 1981. He had joined BTP in 1977 as Assistant Chief Constable, Northern Area. During his term as Chief Constable Mr Ogram fostered good relationships with the Railway Companies and oversaw the development of Force professionalism during such major events as the Miners Strike, the Lockerbie Air Disaster, the Kings Cross Fire, the Clapham and Purley Rail Crashes – what became known as the 'Decade of Disasters'.

1981 also saw the closure of Area Headquarters at Manchester and Bristol, when Force Headquarters moved from Park Royal to new, larger offices at Tavistock Place in London. Three Assistant Chief Constables moved to Force Headquarters, responsible for Administration, Personnel and Training and Operations.

Tavistock Place.

Mr Ogram was to retire from the Force in 1989. He was succeeded by the present Chief Constable Desmond O'Brien, formerly of the Royal Ulster Constabulary, who joined Greater Manchester Police as an Assistant Chief Constable in 1978, and Kent County Constabulary as Deputy Chief Constable in 1983, thus bringing with him a wealth of management and people skills as well as experience.

Directing traffic at Liverpool Lime Street Station.

Chapter Eleven

THE DOCKS AFTER NATIONALISATION

With the passing of the Transport Act in 1947, the vast majority of the country's ports came under the control of the British Transport Commission (BTC). Exceptions were Bristol, Glasgow, Liverpool, London, Tyneside and one or two others that for various reasons remained in private ownership.

Inevitably, some of these changes took time to effect. For instance, the West Riding's 90-year commitment to Goole docks did not end until midnight on 31st July 1954, whereupon a 'Section' of one Sergeant and four Constables of the British Transport Commission Police took over, with Criminal Investigations to be handled by officers from Hull. The docks had previously been policed by a combination of County Police, Special Constables and wartime 'Specials'. The dock authorities looked forward to saving about a thousand pounds a year, with one less officer and BTC pay lower than that of County officers.

Over the next decade the United Kingdom was to lead the world in ship-building, with the docks and ports a haven of activity for industry and tourism. Southampton, which saw the first policewoman added to the strength in 1953, was typical of many. By 1958 it had become a Divisional Police Headquarters led by a Superintendent with over 120 officers. A four-'watch' system operated, i.e. early, shipping, nights and late, with 27 fixed posts to be manned in addition to other duties. The volume of traffic around the docks and the implication and nature of that traffic was such that an officer could not be taken from any of the posts.

A WPC shares a joke with a ship's captain at Southampton Docks.

During the 1950s the great ships *Queen Mary* and *Queen Elizabeth* sailed to and from Southampton every week. Their arrival brought some 1,200 crew and up to 2,000 passengers and visitors. Sergeant Radcliffe, a Constable at the time, described the scene:

'On the "Queen" days practically all available car-parks in the dock are full until the ship's passengers start to leave after the Customs formalities. Apart from crew, passengers and visitors, as soon as these giants dock a host of tradesmen also start their work. On these busy days the police have the problem of dealing with crew members trying to get off the ship as quickly as they can to get home to their wives, the tradesmen trying to get into the ship as quickly as they can to get their work complete, visitors trying all they can to reach their friends, and so on. Sometimes those concerned are hard put to keep an equable temper, but the dock copper is well trained and seldom does he let any situation get the upper hand.'

PC Charlie Cook and Cadet Fred Whitfield.

Other famous visitors to Southampton Docks included the Union Castle Line Ships, *Winchester Castle*, *Carnarvon Castle* and *Stirling Castle*, which provided a weekly service to and from South Africa. Again, arrivals and departures were accompanied by an entourage of visitors, taxis and tradesmen. The Castle Line ships carried between 500 and 1,000 passengers on each trip, as well as cargo, and it was the police officers' duty to 'maintain a calm atmosphere and equilibrium throughout' the time of unloading.

WPC Betty Binns helping passengers on board ship, Southampton Docks.

The Royal Mail Line ships were regulars, among them the passenger- and cargo-carrying RMS *Andes* and *Alcantra*. Elders and Fyffes Ltd, the banana importers, maintained a depot at Southampton, and their ships carried passengers along with their primary cargo. The Ministry of Transport operated troopships from Southampton, and sailings also went to Jersey, St Malo and Le Havre, making it easy for undesirables to ship across from France to this country. Rigid police supervision had to be maintained in conjunction with the Immigration Authority. When the SS *Falaise* and *Normannia* arrived every other morning a minimum of seven police officers were required to control passengers, vehicular traffic, and ensure that every person passed through the Customs and Immigration controls. Each ship had its own peculiarities known to the police and had to be handled in a different way.

During the heyday of the docks Southampton handled half of the country's sea-going passenger traffic. In 1956 nearly 3,000 ships, with a gross tonnage of 21,713,406 tons and a net tonnage of 11,692,928 tons, passed through the port. Outward cargo was about 534,600 tons; 4,022,700 banana stems were handled in the port; 455,160 bags of mail were brought in and 197,898 taken out. 302,510 passengers disembarked and 324,326 passengers embarked. In this kind of environment, where vast numbers of people jostled with each other in the midst of moving machinery, cars, wagons, trains, cranes, wires and ropes, accidents and fatalities were bound to occur. First aid training was vital.

Within the square miles of dockland were a large number of vulnerable properties. In Southampton Docks itself there were several large factories, a fire station, a Rank's mill, workshops, warehouses – bonded and not bonded – canteens, a barber's shop, a laundry shop, sweet and cigarette shops, brewers stores, and others. There was also a passenger flying-boat base; a contingent of RAF personnel; and a US Army base. In order to protect valuable property within the dock area, eight beat systems were devised, with pre-selected 'points' situated near to the emergency telephone boxes. Prior to booking on duty, every Constable was paraded by the duty Section Sergeant and each officer was allocated his beat working or other duty for the day or night. Duties varied for each succeeding watch. Ships being vulnerable to fire, the docks required a twice-nightly fire patrol to be carried out. The Ocean Terminal received special attention and an officer would be detailed to patrol the building as a fire prevention and security measure. In addition, the police office at Southampton Docks had its own miniature telephone exchange, under the control of the 'reserve' officer.

PC Gordon Officer (in uniform) and PC Bill Betteridge.

The increased use of containers on ships helped lessen the cases of pilferage and loss; but problems remained. Whilst conventionally-stored cargo was vulnerable, goods could at least be seen and identified, and losses noticed. With containers, only some of which were sealed, the cargo was extremely difficult to monitor.

In the early 1960s police dogs were added to the strength: 'Chance', 'Rinty', 'Rex VII' and 'Blackie', who between them provided a 24-hour patrol under the watchful eye of Inspector Longland.

Sergeant Duncan Ross, March 1966.

During the Falklands Conflict of 1982, Southampton was the principal commercial port for the departure of commercial liners (*QE2*, *Canberra* and *Uganda*) and of cargo ships to the war zone. For those who had lived through World War II the activity on the docks must have brought back unhappy memories, but for younger generations, this was like nothing they had ever seen. Whilst ships underwent conversion to vessels of war, Chenuke helicopters and trucks were bringing in stores of military equipment, field guns, artillery, vehicles, not to mention over 5,000 troops. Charlie Cook, at that time a Sergeant, recalled seeing boxes and boxes of pickled walnuts waiting to be shipped out to the war zone – something of an oddity amongst the paraphernalia of war. It was almost unreal, like a film set, he said, a feeling perpetuated by the fact that few people even knew where the Falklands were. Extra police officers had to be mobilised to deal with the heightened security risk and increased movements within the docks area, working many hours over-time to handle the load.

Emotions ran high when, a few months later, the *Canberra* and *QE2* returned with triumphant troops and such 'trophies' as Argentinean planes. At one time, around 30,000 people filled the docks, with military bands playing and a carnival-like atmosphere that was vastly different from the heavy, tense days in which the troops had left.

The QE2 arrives back in Southampton at the end of the Falklands Conflict.
Courtesy of The Southern Daily Echo.

The risk of oil pollution led to the Oil in Navigable Waters Act of 1955 which restricted the discharge of oil from shipping, land installations, etc., in territorial and inland waters of the UK. BTP Docks Police took samples of oil from docks and from ships suspected of the spillage.

HULL DOCKS

Situated as it is on the doorstep of the industrial North East and within easy reach of the continent of Europe, Hull from its earliest days maintained a thriving fishing and trading fleet. In the 19th century the railway companies realised its value as a commercial port and undertook considerable development of the area. St Andrews Dock was at one time acknowledged as one of the world's largest fishing ports, hundreds of tons of fish being distributed daily by train to all parts of the country, and most of the city dependent on the waterfront and its allied trades for their livelihood. The whole of this vast docks area was policed initially by Railway Police, and later British Transport Police. The busy Hull Division comprised over 100 officers, including those stationed at Goole Docks, some 23 miles inland along the Humber.

One ever-present source of concern were the prostitutes who frequented the area. The Street Offences Act of 1959 did not apply in the docks, so prostitutes were generally charged with 'trespassing' and prosecuted under the Dock Bye-law. Invariably the maximum fine of £5 was imposed, to be paid there and then, the alternative being 30 days imprisonment. Dealing with smuggling, theft of cargo, serious assaults between crew members, stowaways, recalcitrant seamen and prostitutes, also kept officers busy and they had to be as well versed in Shipping Acts as they were with those of the railways.

THE PORT OF WEYMOUTH

Like the ports, coastal towns developed their own culture and officers have fond memories of their service there. During the early 1970s Keith Groves was stationed at Weymouth as a Detective Constable. Together with one Sergeant and five Constables, he policed Bournemouth, the New Forest and the Channel Island routes, where tomato thefts were a particular problem. Officers worked closely with

Customs and Excise, checking on crews returning from the Islands where duty-free goods were so much cheaper. The laws on the Islands dictate that if residents are destitute or commit an offence, they should be deported for three years. If they commit again, they are deported for life. In cases such as these, the Island police would inform police officers who, in turn, would board the ferries and remove the individual before other passengers disembarked.

Weymouth was also famous for its boat-train. On reaching the sidings at Weymouth from Waterloo, the train joined the town's tram lines. At this point it was necessary for a police car or police motorcycle to escort it through the town's streets. Railwaymen known as 'Shunters' walked in front, directing the train with flags. Parked cars obstructing the train had to be man-handled out of the way, and their owners fined.

PC Gerry Gerrard, based at Portsmouth, is the Home Beat Officer for the Isle of Wight, the BTP's only island police officer. Island Line, the Isle of Wight's train operating unit, has eight miles of track and eight stations. PC Gerrard, who works closely with Hampshire police, deals with incidents of trespass, criminal damage to stations and some minor order offences associated with seaside resorts.

STRANRAER

Between 1980 and 1984, an annual average of 95,000 passengers passed through Stranraer on their way to Ireland. Inspector Alec Harris described the type of policing that was required there.

'One of the busiest times for the port was during the Orange Marching Season around the 12th July, when Orange Lodge marching bands would travel across from Larne to Stranraer and Scottish bands would travel from Stranraer to Larne. The Sealink ferries *Antrim Princess* and the *Aisla Princess* carried these bands and a police presence of one sergeant and up to six constables would be required to travel on the two and a half hour crossing for the purpose of reassurance and control of behaviour. Football supporters travelling to and from

Northern Ireland for International and League matches also provided us with plenty of work. During the crossings we would do our best to keep the rival fans in separate areas of the ship.'

As with many ports around the country, apprehending 'ladies of the night' kept officers busy. One frequent visitor to Stranraer during Harris's time was 'Diesel Lil'. Police officers were forever removing her from the port area, whereupon she would sneak into the back of a lorry and have herself smuggled back in. Other smuggled goods included whisky – a notorious problem around the Scottish Coast, although less so today as a result of the work of Customs and Excise officers. In addition to their own duties, BTP officers would be required to keep a vigilant eye out for suspicious-looking boats and cargo.

Stranraer Railway Station is situated at the end of the pier, so officers would divide their time between the trains and the ferries. During the summer season, sleeper and excursion trains run regularly from Stranraer, making the area busy with tourists. The port is also a through-route for cars on their way from manufacturers in the south of England to showrooms in Ireland. Officers were required to patrol yards and lines, as the shiny metal was a constant temptation for vandals to dent and scratch, whilst radios and other car fittings were vulnerable to theft. Incidences of theft also arose from the passage of mail bags to Ireland, the number rising dramatically in the pre-Christmas months.

HEYSHAM HARBOUR

Heysham Harbour is a busy port on the North West Coast of England. Chief Inspector John Leyland was transferred there as a cadet back in May of 1970, when a new terminal was being built and existing ferries converted to transfer cars and passengers to Belfast on a nightly service. It was a period of great expansion for the port and in line with this, under the watchful eye of Inspector George Smith Leach, the police establishment grew considerably. In time they were provided with a police station inside the new terminal building. With the increase in IRA terrorist activity on mainland Britain, Heysham was targeted as a major through-point and therefore became subject to top security measures.

The duties at Heysham were varied. Not only were officers policing the ferries and their terminal, they also policed Sealink-owned steamers on Lake Windermere, *The Swan, The Teal, The Turn* and *The Swift*, which ran during the summer months and on Bank Holidays. There was a tendency among some passengers to remain 'propping up the bar' of the steamers all day, with alcohol-induced behaviour requiring extra police attention.

Heysham is also surrounded by a busy rail network, and Leyland recalls working 14-hour night shifts on the Travelling Post Office trains from Whitehaven to Huddersfield.

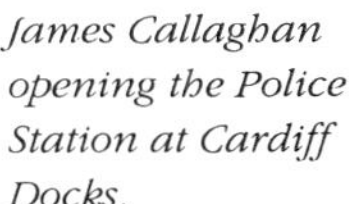

James Callaghan opening the Police Station at Cardiff Docks.

HMS Churchill, a nuclear powered visitor to the Queens Pier Head Lock, Cardiff Docks, 1973. Whenever such vessels were in the docks, a huge supply of 'emergency' anti-radiation pills were retained at the Docks Police Station.

THE MINERS STRIKE SIT-IN AT PORT TALBOT DOCKS

Between August and September 1984 the BTP were involved in the mineworkers' occupation of three dockside cranes at Port Talbot Docks, South Wales, where coal and iron ore from around the world was being unloaded for supply to the British Steel Corporation.

On the evening of Thursday 30th August the Spanish vessel *MV Argos* arrived in port carrying 96,000 tons of coal. As it did so, a convoy of 14 hired vans and private cars approached a barrier, guarded by a single BSC security officer. The officer attempted to warn his control office, but was prevented by several men descending upon him and tearing the radio out. A second security officer approached the barrier and attempted to stop the vehicles, but one of them struck him twice and he was forced to step out of the way as they drove on past him.

The cars stopped, and strikers emerged and began climbing up the catwalks of the cranes which were being prepared for unloading. The foreman spotted them and ordered his crane drivers out of their cabs and into a position of safety. Now in an elevated and advantageous position, the strikers began hurling metal objects down onto the deck. Another striker cast adrift one of the boats used to bring mooring lines to the jetty. The Captain of the *MV Argos*, having witnessed all this, ordered the gangway to be lifted and for his own men to move into a position of safety.

Inspector David Thomas of South Wales Police was the first officer on the scene, closely followed by Constables Williams and Prosser of BTP, who were instructed to observe from the jetty. A number of other supporting officers arrived, including Inspector Livesley and Superintendent Ayres, all of whom witnessed chanting and the throwing of missiles on to the jetty. Flood lights were set up to illuminate the scene.

Despite foul weather and high winds, by daybreak some of the strikers had barricaded themselves onto the scaffold. They informed Inspector Livesley that they would remain in their positions until the ship was removed. In subsequent exchanges the group identified themselves as the South Wales Miners Union representing 28 Welsh lodges. ACC Ian McGregor (Operations) arrived at the scene soon after and took charge of the operation; he decided that police officers should not attempt to climb the cranes but should sit it out and wait for the strikers to come down.

At midday on 31st August a coach carrying around 45 miners arrived at the docks. Having been refused entry, a number of the men got off the coach and stormed past the lock gates on their way towards the jetty. Before reaching it they were approached by seven officers and a vehicle carrying PC Beddoe and his dog 'Major'. On hearing Major barking inside, the miners' mood changed and they were escorted back muttering 'We don't mind arguing with you but we're not messing about with the dog!'

That same day Committee Members of the NUM along with the Union Solicitors, arrived at the docks to negotiate an end to the take-over. ACC McGregor informed the delegation that no conditions were to be negotiated and that when the men came down they would be arrested and dealt with according to the law. A couple of hours later officers on the bridge of the *MV Argos* saw the men on the cranes placing more barbed wire around the steps.

The situation continued on through most of Saturday, with further incidents of missile throwing and attempts at negotiation by NUM leaders and their solicitors. Finally, just before 5 p.m., an NUM Representative advised the police that the men would be down in 15 minutes. As each man came down, he was arrested and taken to one of five police stations for documentation, search and interview.

A vast number of missiles were subsequently retrieved for evidence, and the damage caused was estimated at £9,265. The take-over had been organised by officials at both Welsh National and Lodge level of the National Union of Mineworkers. It transpired that the local press had been aware of the incident two hours before it occurred, having been briefed by NUM representatives. At the subsequent trial, the Judge, Mr Justice Leonard, commended BTP for the way they had handled the situation, saying:

'I think you behaved with considerable restraint. It may be that to some extent it was a case of discretion being the better part of valour, but I think to a more important extent it was a case of good sense and good police work. If there had been a confrontation there would, in my view, almost certainly have been very much more serious trouble, and perhaps I would be sitting here trying a very much more serious case.'

Ninety-nine miners received suspended sentences of six months'; two received immediate sentences of six months in jail; and one was conditionally discharged for two years.

THE DECLINE OF THE SHIPPING INDUSTRY

The last thirty years have seen many changes on the docks and ports of Britain. As other countries introduced more automation to their ship yards, so the UK's position slipped to eighth position, resulting in unemployment and a shift from industry to tourism.

In 1962 the British Transport Docks Board (BTDB) was created, responsible for 'Deep water berths'; whilst British Railways Board (BRB) retained the smaller passenger ferry ports under the title of British Railway Shipping International Services. In January 1979 Sealink UK was founded, a wholly owned subsidiary of BRB, which took on the ferry ports and the ferries themselves. The BTDB changed its name in 1983 to Associated British Ports (ABP).

Patrolling the docks, 1966.

In 1985, having survived nationalisation and the steady decline of the shipyards, the BTP finally lost their jurisdiction over the docks. For economic reasons, Associated British Ports had decided to relinquish the services of the Force, resulting in the deployment of 270 officers to other areas. Sealink followed suit in 1989. It was a traumatic time as many officers had served on the docks throughout their career. Some chose to take early retirement, whilst other officers relocated to the London areas where they had the opportunity to prove their worth in a more challenging environment than the docks had become. In view of Dr Beeching's railway cut-backs of the 1960s, when the thriving docks had absorbed so many of the officers, it seemed ironic that tables had now turned.

Chapter Twelve

SPECIAL MOVEMENTS

The chief responsibility of BTP's 'Special Movements' Department is the Royal Train, on which members of the Royal Family travel regularly, and ensuring that there is minimum fuss and inconvenience to the travelling public during major events. Essentially part of the Royal household, the train can be closely monitored and patrolled, and therefore avoids the security problems involved in staying at hotels. On board, BTP officers have their own compartment and a designated escort vehicle. Their self-contained communications room, which is constantly in use, informs local forces of their position, so that preparations can be made, particularly when stopping at a station. Once searched, a station will be kept 'sterile', i.e. access restricted; the destination point is also kept 'secure', as is the stabling point where the train stops overnight. Staff work in close liaison with the Force Search Advisor and the Royal Protection Officers. The Special Movements Department has existed in some form or another since 1842, when the very first railway journey was made by a British reigning Monarch. The occasion took place on 13th June, with Queen Victoria and the Prince Consort travelling on the Great Western Railway from Slough (the nearest station to her home at Windsor Castle) to Paddington. Hauled by an engine bearing the nameplate

Phlegethon, and driven by its designer Mr D Gooch, Queen Victoria's train comprised a second class 'brake' carriage, a saloon or 'posting' carriage, the Queen's saloon, a second 'posting' carriage and three 'carriage' trucks for household staff and baggage. The GWR Police afforded protection to Her Majesty under the auspices of Mr Collard, the Great Western's first Chief of Police. Having previously only travelled by horse-drawn carriage and accustomed to the stares and the cat-calls of bystanders, it was not surprising that, on arrival in London, Her Majesty expressed herself as being 'quite charmed at the privacy and lack of dust.' For services rendered during her reign, the GWR Police were invited to wear a crown on their badge.

Inspector Ken Avis, together with Peter Richardson, a member of the Royal Train Staff, and the Station Manager London (Victoria).

The following year the Queen made several more journeys: to Gosport on the London & South Western Railway, in order to cross to her country home at Osborne in the Isle of Wight, and to various parts of the Midlands on the London & Birmingham Railway. She made her first long distance journey on 28th September 1848 – from Balmoral in Scotland to London. Journeys to and from the Royal retreat had previously been made in the Royal Yacht, but adverse weather conditions on this occasion brought a request for a Royal Train. At a few hours' notice, the Aberdeen Railway Company had a train ready at Montrose. The journey to London included two overnight stops at Perth and Crewe, where the Queen stayed in local hotels. During the Fenian outrages of the mid to late 19th century, fears for the Queen's safety resulted in officers being posted within sight of each other along the route from Windsor to Balmoral.

The locomotives which hauled the Royal Trains were always the latest the Railway Companies could provide and would often be decorated with bunting, flags and the Royal Coat of Arms. The London Brighton & South Coast Railway even went so far as to whitewash the coal in the tender, improving appearance and dowsing the dust! Apparently the Queen objected to travelling at more than 40 miles per hour and, ironically, the fastest journey she ever made was to her own funeral. She died at Osbourne on 22nd January 1901, with the Royal Train carrying her body from Gosport to Victoria Station via the London, Brighton & South Coast Railway and from there on to Paddington and Windsor via the Great Western.

Such was the regard with which the Railway Police were held, that in June 1912, when King George V and Queen Mary visited Cardiff for four days in the Royal Yacht *Alexandra*, they presented Superintendent Davies of the Bute Docks Police with a ruby tie pin as a token of their appreciation. Davies accepted the gift on behalf of the Inspector, eight Sergeants and 36 Constables of the Force.

A Railway Policeman watches over King George V and Queen Mary at Bolton Station during the Royal tour of Lancashire, 1913. Courtesy of Science & Society Picture Library.

THE CORONATION OF HM QUEEN ELIZABETH II

For the British Transport Commission Police preparations for the Coronation of Queen Elizabeth II on 2nd June 1953 began as early as September 1952. As the event drew closer the city was decorated with flags, bunting and lights, and increasingly large crowds of people travelled into the city every day to see them. VIP arrivals culminated on 30th and 31st May 1953 with more than 50 arriving at Victoria on one train alone – 'Princes, Princesses, Royal Highnesses and Imperial Highnesses, Comtes, Very Reverends, Dons, Sheiks, Senors, Barons etc. from almost unheard of places, Laos, Cambodia, Kuwait, Qatar, besides those from Europe and Arabia, Liechtenstein, Holy See, Lebanon, etc. etc.', the Journal reports – all of whom were welcomed by the Duke of Edinburgh on the platform. That evening fireworks displays brought ever more crowds into the city, all of whom needed to get home a few hours later. Heavy rain did not succeed in dampening people's spirits, and though wet and tired, travellers remained law-abiding.

The Journal talks of

'Every available policeman, working, it seemed, every hour of the day and night, as happy as the crowds and as tired, getting people home up to the "late" early hours of the next morning, the 3rd. And on the 3rd 100 of them with contingents from other Areas lined the streets of the City of London, when Her Majesty passed through on her State Drive.'

Officers on parade at the Coronation of Queen Elizabeth II.

On Coronation day itself, special trains started arriving from 3.00 a.m. onwards. Shortly after 6.00 a.m., some 900 school children arrived at Waterloo to be marshalled over Hungerford Bridge – they were the only ones allowed to use the bridge that day. Meanwhile 150 British Transport Commission Police officers paraded at St Paul's Gardens to be inspected by Chief Officer W B Richards MVO, accompanied by Colonel Nick Jesper DSO, OBE, MC, prior to taking up positions in Cheapside for the Queen's State Drive to the Guildhall.

On 9th June the Queen attended a Thanksgiving Service at St Paul's Cathedral, with 100 officers of the British Transport Commission Police from all over England and Wales, together with London Transport Executive officers, helping to control the crowds as they lined the streets outside hoping for a sight of the new Queen.

The event was a great success for all concerned. Commissioner A E Young of the City of London Police wrote to Colonel Jesper:

'I want to take this, the earliest opportunity, of expressing my sincere thanks and appreciation for the help so readily and efficiently given by the members of the British Transport Commission Police, who turned out to assist us on the 3rd and the 9th June, and again today.

In view of our depleted strength, the help was doubly welcome. We were delighted to have them with us and I should be so glad if you could convey my personal thanks to those Officers and Constables who formed the contingents.

We shall not hesitate to seek your help on further public occasions.'

THE BRITISH EMPIRE AND COMMONWEALTH GAMES

Between 18th and 26th July 1958 the British Empire and Commonwealth Games were held in Cardiff, Wales. It was an occasion without parallel for the BTCP who patrolled Cardiff's railways and docks. No less than 101,000 employees of the National Coal Board, on holiday at the time, arrived by car, coach and train to watch the games; and in addition to the other visitors, there were a number of members of the Royal Family who arrived by Royal Train or Royal Yacht. For the four days *Britannia* was berthed in the docks, security measures were extremely tight, with extra officers drafted in to handle the workload. Fortunately it was a relatively crime-free time as the only recorded arrest is of a docker caught stealing paint!

Chief Inspector W Voyle talked in the Journal of how BTCP officers were solely responsible for the security of the Royal Yacht during its stay, for all of the traffic arrangements and for the 101 things which a royal visit of some duration obviously entails. Cardiff Docks has a complicated network of roadways, including over 20 miles of metalled roads. The roads weave round and over the docks and with a uniform strength at Cardiff Docks of 38 men, the first consideration was to establish the number of officers that would be required. Superintendent Leath wisely decided at the outset that it was not possible to over-estimate what might happen. It was decided to import 45 officers to augment the men in the Division; and at the height of the activities arising out of the royal visit, and in addition to normal police duties, there were some 90 men fully engaged at Cardiff Docks, Cardiff General Station and Cardiff Queen Street Station.

Many meetings were held to work out the details. Each officer performing duty was issued with a set of instructions consisting of 13 foolscap pages and a duty roster which ran into some 24 foolscap pages. To overcome the lack of local knowledge of the visiting officers, a special diagrammatic plan was prepared of the docks, with every officer supplied a copy.

The officers carried out their duties in a most worthy manner, Voyle reported. One of the most unusual assignments was given to PC Hopkins (Taunton), a well-known water polo player and a Somerset County Cap, who was posted in the vicinity of Roath Basin for the express purpose of rescuing anybody who fell into the dock

With the traditional resourcefulness of police officers, a wooden hut was discovered in the civil engineers' yard at the docks and was erected at a strategic point. This eventually became known as the Royal Yacht Police Office. On one occasion somebody telephoned and asked 'Is that the Yacht Club?' Sleeping accommodation was provided in railway coaches at Bute Road Station and two prefabricated huts were erected on the site for the comfort and convenience of visiting officers.

A real innovation was the use of walkie-talkies. A visit was paid to the Signal Department at Reading where two master sets and six walkie-talkies were discovered. Within a week all the equipment was transferred to Cardiff Docks and experiments in their use soon began. The Cardiff policewomen took to the walkie-talkies like veterans. After only a few hours' practice they were on the air. When the time came, to the amazement of the Captain of the Royal Yacht, he was given a running commentary of the movements of HRH the Duke of Edinburgh from the time he left the boxing at Sophia Gardens until he reached the main entrance at Cardiff Docks on his way to join the *Britannia* on 25th July. This was achieved as a result of messages transmitted from a Cardiff City Police car to the information room at the City Headquarters, then over direct line from the information room to the Cardiff Docks police office and over the walkie-talkie link-up to the gangway of the Royal Yacht. 'The equipment was invaluable,' Voyle said.

To the officers on the docks the highlight of the use of the walkie-talkie equipment was the visit of Mr K W C Grand, General Manager of the Western Region and a member of the Police Committee. Mr Grand's visit coincided with the departure of HRH the Duke of Edinburgh from the yacht to the Cardiff City Civic Centre. Mr Grand's car was directed by Cardiff City Police into a side street, and was rescued by BTP officers at the main gate of the docks. It was known at the control point that Mr Grand was on his way to the docks and a message was sent through the walkie-talkie to the main gate. Mr Grand arrived at the Yacht Police Office some five minutes before the Duke left the yacht and thus had a first-hand experience of the effectiveness of the walkie-talkie system. It was also necessary to advise the Cardiff City Police immediately the Duke left the yacht and this was also done through the walkie-talkies.

Transport within the docks was an important factor. Members of the Western Area Mobile Squad were formed into a pool of drivers and a 20-seater bus was borrowed to convey parties of men to various points around the docks – although Officers first had to qualify as public service vehicle drivers. As a departure from the routine of police duty, visiting officers were taken on conducted tours of the City of Cardiff.

The opportunity to walk the decks of the Royal Yacht was granted to the policewomen stationed at Cardiff at the special invitation of the Yacht Captain. At all times there was a very good liaison between the officers of the yacht and the BTC police officers, particularly, Voyle remembers, as they had a mutual interest in the floral decorations of the Yacht Police Office!

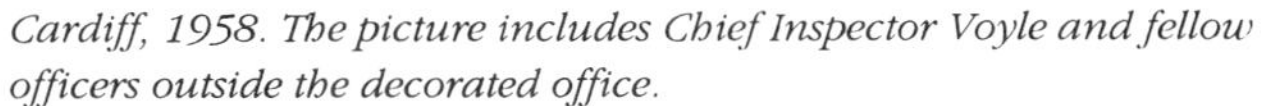

Cardiff, 1958. The picture includes Chief Inspector Voyle and fellow officers outside the decorated office.

Among the services rendered was the provision of a pilot car for Rear Admiral Dawnay, Flag Officer, Royal Yacht, on his various trips around the docks. This duty was performed by Sergeant Hickox and PC Smith, and the officers received the personal thanks of the Rear Admiral who was amazed at the complexity of the roads on the docks.

At 6.15 p.m. on 26th July 1958, at the Queen's Pier Head, HM Yacht *Britannia* slipped her mooring ropes and gently moved out of the docks into the Bristol Channel to the cheers of thousands of people. The departure marked the end of four hectic days and two months of detailed planning.

THE QUEEN'S SILVER JUBILEE

The Queen's Silver Jubilee on 12th June 1977 was a huge, national celebration, involving many members of the BTP, as well as other Forces. The crowds began gathering on the pavements during the night of 11th June, but were all in good spirits by morning time. On taking up their places, and on the final stand later in the afternoon, the men and women of the various Forces received cheers and applause. Police raincoats – fortunately not needed – were handed over to members of the crowd to look after, and not one went missing!

As the procession made its way through the streets, there were special cheers for the Queen Mother and for the Queen's Royal Canadian Mounted Police escort, rising to a crescendo as the Queen and Prince Philip passed in the Gold State Coach followed by Prince Charles on horseback. It was a great day.

Chief Superintendent Gerry Lee, the City of London Officer-in-Charge, praised the officers on duty, saying:

'That everything went so well was largely due to the efficient, courteous and considerate way in which the police handled the crowds. The British Transport Police were a very great help and their efficiency and smartness were favourably commented upon by the crowds, who asked questions about the various forces assisting us.'

HM Queen Elizabeth II opening Euston Station, 14th October 1968.

Officers on parade, 1968.

THE FUNERAL OF EARL MOUNTBATTEN

The funeral of Earl Mountbatten on 5th September 1979 was the largest operation of its kind ever mounted by the Force. Mountbatten's relationship with the British and several foreign Royal Families gave rise to the largest gathering of royalty in one place for many years, and this, together with the IRA connection with his death, meant the procession was an obvious target for further terrorist attacks. Altogether there were close to 180 uniformed and CID officers on duty, as well as a huge Metropolitan contingent who assisted by lining part of the route to Waterloo Station.

Following planning meetings and rehearsals, work proper began on the eve of the event, when the train that would carry the coffin to the Earl's home town of Romsey for a private internment ceremony, was placed under police guard at Stewart's Lane carriage sheds. At the same time officers began clearing Waterloo Station of cars that might pose a security risk or obstruction, whilst any persons found loitering were questioned and kept under observation.

On the morning of the Funeral a team of CID officers and technical staff made an inch by inch search of the train's interior and exterior before it left, still under police guard, for Waterloo. At Clapham Junction the police radio coach that had been coupled to the Royal Train, bringing the Royal Family from Balmoral to Euston, was now coupled to the Funeral Train and equipped with fresh radio operators. BTP officers, aided by railway engineers, checked tunnels as well as platforms.

The train arrived at Waterloo on Platform 11, in the middle of the 'controlled zone'. A series of check points sealed off the area, with only authorised persons gaining admittance, still under observation. 'Screen trains' were placed on Platforms 10 and 12, which extended the controlled zone still further. CID officers, wearing boiler suits and hard hats, examined the route in minute detail as well as the controlled zone and all nearby or overlooking premises. Roofs, subways, offices – anywhere terrorists could act – were all searched by officers and dogs from both BTP and Metropolitan Police Forces.

Barriers had been erected on the concourse, and uniformed officers kept spectators much further away from the procession than usual; they stood facing them, backed up by officers in observation posts on roofs and other vantage points. Others mingled with the crowds. Outside the station, uniformed officers kept traffic on the move until road closures in the vicinity dried up the flow.

All incidents were dealt with quickly, quietly and efficiently; they included a hoax call about a bomb in a litter bin; a man purporting to be a member of the 'Tokyo Terrorist Group'; and another man who began heckling the crowd as the procession passed him. All proved harmless.

Leaving Westminster Abbey almost 20 minutes late, the procession headed for Waterloo – a police-escorted Royal Navy bearer party; a Metropolitan Police motor cycle escort, an armoured car escort, the Land Rover carrying the coffin, and, finally, 19 cars and two buses of mourners, including four crowned Heads of State. They arrived at the hushed station where two early morning rehearsals had ensured that the placing of the coffin on the train, the entraining of the mourners, and the positioning of the armoured cars and other vehicles, were carried out with split second timing, and in a stately, dignified manner.

At the pre-arranged time of 1255 hours, the train departed. Aboard, Inspector Keith Meager and two officers of the Royal Protection team were armed, and, along with other uniformed and CID officers, remained alert for the slightest hint of trouble. Throughout the journey radio contact was maintained with the driver's cab, senior railway officials on the train, as well as with the helicopter that shadowed the train along its route. HQ operators radioed progress on their multi-channel set to the Metropolitan, Surrey and Hampshire Forces. Ninety-five minutes later the train arrived at Romsey where 'D' (Southampton) Division took over, having themselves made an equal amount of preparation. All of the officers involved on the day experienced one of their most emotional tours of duty.

The cortege arrives at Waterloo.

Later that evening, most of the Royal Family returned to London by car, but Princess Anne and a number of other dignitaries returned in the train. A high level of security was maintained, but there was little ceremony on arrival at Waterloo, with Lord Chamberlain's staff guiding passengers quickly and quietly to their cars. The vehicles drove rapidly out of the station, between large crowds of people attracted to the scene by the police cordons, and members of BTP returned to their normal duties.

Preparations for Prince Charles's visit to Halifax Station, December 1987.

The Duchess of Kent arriving at North Allerton, 1993.

STATE VISITS, VIP AND CELEBRITY MOVEMENTS

State visits by foreign dignitaries have always been important, public occasions, featuring much pomp and ceremony. *The Illustrated London News* of 16th and 21st April 1855 devoted its pages to the State visit of the Emperor Napoleon of France, and his Imperial Consort the Empress Eugenie.

'The preparations of the worthy burgesses of Dover for the reception of their illustrious visitors had been completed early in the morning. Triumphal arches appeared, duly decked with verdant laurel, Imperial cyphers had been wrought in choice flowers, and naval, military and civic dignitaries were all arrayed in their best, and panting with nervous eagerness to do the honours in their several departments.

This place was strictly guarded by the militia, and a long boarded platform, covered with crimson cloth, stretched from it all along the Admiralty pier to the landing place. The platform was, of course, strongly palisadoed on both sides, and strictly kept by the police; but still the crowd pressed densely.'

Today, officers of the British Transport Police are involved in State visits around twice yearly. In addition to high level security training, members of the Special Movements Department must be extremely well versed in the political situation of this and other countries, in order to assess the threat level to a foreign visitor during his stay in the UK. Dignitaries arrive at Gatwick Airport or Victoria Station by Royal Train, where they are met by senior members of the Royal Family or cabinet ministers. In 1995 it became the norm for Her Majesty The Queen to greet State visitors in Horse Guards Parade. Prior to general elections, government ministers are also active on the railway; Margaret Thatcher had her very own train, for which the BTP, was also responsible.

Waterloo Station, September 1956. The arrival of American pianist Liberace required the services of 12 BTP officers to clear a way through the crowds for his car. These scenes were a regular feature when celebrities crossed the Atlantic by liner to Southampton and travelled on to Waterloo by boat train.

The Queen and President of Brazil receive the Royal Salute, 1976.

In 1985 Live Aid, the huge concert organised by Bob Geldof in aid of the victims of famine in Ethiopia, involved some 80 BTP officers in and around Wembley Stadium. Celebrities were transported to the stadium throughout the course of the day in helicopters, landing in a London Transport-owned sports pavilion at the rear of the stadium, where a cricket match was being played and a wedding reception held. The match had to be halted each time a helicopter landed, with celebrities moved over to a huge caravan, from where they were able to watch play continue whilst awaiting transport through to the stadium.

Royal Weddings and such events as the VE and VJ day celebrations in 1995 continue to involve the Force, as do all movements of explosive substances, both military and commercial.

Inspector Michael Foster and Rick Parfitt of Status Quo at Live Aid.

Chapter Thirteen

CRIMINAL INVESTIGATIONS

THE GREAT TRAIN ROBBERY

Investigations into serious theft on the railways have always come under the remit of the British Transport Police Criminal Investigations Department. Over the years the scale and nature of theft has grown and changed considerably. In the early 1960s, for example, there was a trend among some lorry drivers to 'divert' cargos of whisky or tobacco en route between stations and depots. 'Dragging' was a method of covert surveillance whereby CID officers tracked them across town or Channel and acted on incidents they witnessed.

Probably the most infamous railway theft of all was the Great Train Robbery on 8th August 1963. By altering the line signal near Bridego Bridge, north of London, 15 robbers led by Bruce Reynolds brought the Glasgow to London Royal Mail train to a complete halt, and lifted from it over £2.5 million worth of used bank notes in 120 mail bags. They fled to pre-arranged refuge in a Buckinghamshire farmhouse, where they divided the cash amongst themselves, congratulated themselves on a job well done, and then dispersed to various parts of the country. Unfortunately for them, not every part of the job was well done: they had arranged for the farmhouse to be burned down and the evidence destroyed, but the arsonists bungled their work and the investigating police officers of Buckinghamshire, BTP and the Metropolitan, were able to identify every one of the gang members by his fingerprints. Twelve of the 15 robbers were subsequently caught, convicted and received prison sentences. Of these, Ronnie Biggs managed to escape in 1965 and, in doing so, attained near celebrity status.

Mail bags have been a constant temptation for thieves since mail was first carried by rail in 1838.

The robbery highlighted the vulnerability of Royal Mail Trains, and resulted in the Government requesting that, from 1964 onwards, all journeys be accompanied by BTP officers wearing protective gear and communications equipment. In the event of the train making an unscheduled stop – at signals for example – the position would be radioed through to a controller, the train's air vents closed and gas masks held at the ready for use in case of an attack. This remained the practice until 1973 when new, more economic measures were enforced.

REGIONAL CRIME SQUADS

In the 1960s a large number of serious criminals were evading police forces by moving from one area to another. Also, policing tended to be re-active – i.e. responding to crimes committed – not pro-active – i.e. taking preventative action. To tackle the issue, Regional Crime Squads (RCSs) were set up, with officers of a number of forces joining together to target problem offenders across police boundaries. Many joint operations have since been conducted by officers of the BTP and Regional Crime Squads, and one BTP officer is now permanently seconded to train officers from all Forces on RCS courses.

SPECIALIST SQUADS

Following the Great Train Robbery, thieves continued to employ innovative means by which to foil police officers. One thief used to hide himself in a large aluminium trunk, wearing an oxygen mask so that he could breathe, and have himself delivered to railway stations where he would be placed on the train with the mail bags. During the journey he would climb out of the trunk through a trap door, grab a few mail bags and crawl back inside with them. By the time he was caught, he had lifted around £200,000 worth of property in this way.

With thefts of high value mail on the increase, there was a growing trend towards the hiring of private security firms; however, the problem continued to get worse and in the late 1960s, three specialist squads were set up, under the control of a Detective Chief Superintendent. They specialised in:

1.   Stations & Depots – dealing with large scale thefts.
2.   Mail Bags – dealing with thefts of high value mail.
3.   Dining Car Fraud – dealing with thefts of money and goods.

Three highly respected officers led the squads, as well as having overcall command of the CID on a national basis: Basil Nichols, Maurice Woodman and the late John Innes, who was particularly skilled in liaising with the Post Office. They and the men who served under them brought great professionalism to investigative procedures, although occasionally things did not go according to plan. In the early '80s, Detective Constable Glyde and his colleagues were investigating a series of high value thefts from trains at Basingstoke when they were rather surprised to spot a vicar making off with a number of mail bags. They moved forward to apprehend him; but a tackle turned into a fight when two old ladies, each armed with a rather sharp and heavy umbrella, decided to join in – on the side of the vicar, whom of course they presumed to be innocent. The 'vicar' turned out to be a professional actor who had, by this time, misappropriated £100,000 worth of post office mail.

During an investigation at Romford police dogs were sent into a brake carriage ahead of officers to round up a team of thieves armed with knives; the thieves were duly caught and arrested; however, in the process, a combination of knives, teeth and claws managed to shred the protected mail!

Another thief who managed to evade the police time and time again, eventually came to a sticky end of his own accord. Having broken into the Guards van, he threw the mail bags out of the train, and then himself after them. Unfortunately for him a series of wooden stakes were fencing the track. Later, officers arriving at the scene took little time to work out that the body impaled on a stake and surrounded by mail bags belonged to the man they had been searching for some time in connection with a number of thefts.

By far the biggest investigation – handled jointly by all three squads and involving liaison with law enforcement agencies around the world – was to uncover thefts of over £2 million worth of property. The investigation ran from 1981 to 1983, and was led by Detective Chief Superintendent Woodman, and assisted by Detective Constable Cousins, Detective Constable Glyde and Superintendent Satchwell. Arrests produced the largest ever number of defendants to stand together in the Old Bailey charged with conspiracy to fraud. Of those eventually convicted were Tom Wisby, one of the Great Train Robbers, Billy Gentry, Jack Mullins and Phil Jacobs, all well known villains in the City.

In late 1993 Detective Inspector Alan Pacey led an investigation into a particular spate of mail bag robberies in the London area that was to result in the recovery of £30 million worth of vehicle excise licences. The investigation culminated in an undercover operation in which officers disguised as gangsters arranged to meet with a team of four individuals outside a fast-food restaurant in London, where it was agreed they would 'purchase' a consignment of licences for £80,000. The four men produced several carrier bags full of the licences – and were accordingly arrested.

During 1994/95 a further spate of thefts in London resulted in the mounting of undercover operation 'Sting'. In order to indicate to the Courts that the suspects were persistent offenders, a bogus trading premises was set up and manned by officers posing as gang members. The officers were repeatedly approached by 16 suspects who offered to sell them stolen property. During the course of the operation several hundred stolen credit cards were retrieved, along with around £30,000 worth of property.

DIP SQUADS

Since the early days of rail travel, plain clothes officers have been tackling the problem of 'Dips' – professional pickpockets who haunt London Underground in particular, stealing bags, purses and wallets from unsuspecting passengers. They often work in teams, one of them jamming open the train door whilst an accomplice grabs the item and within a matter of seconds passes it to a third accomplice who makes off with it. When challenged, the Dips rarely give up without a fight, which, next to live rails, can be extremely dangerous. Armed with crime pattern experience and by observing suspects' behaviour, teams of Dip Squad officers were set up during the 1970s to tackle the problem. Detective Sergeant Gregory was a major influence behind the success of Dip Squads, and his experience was well respected throughout BTP and other Forces.

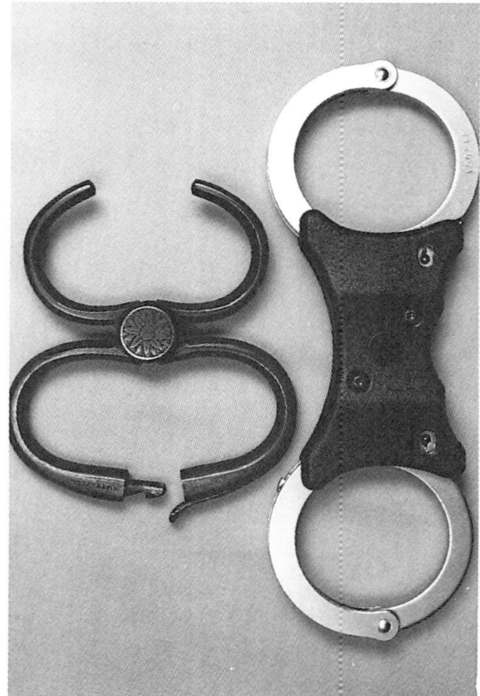

[far left] These handcuffs from the early 1900s were commonly used on the docks, where the offender may have been arrested some distance from the police office. Their design made it difficult for a villain to put up much of a fight.

Handcuffs were issued generally throughout the Force during the early 1960s. There have been several designs, all made by Hyatts of Birmingham, culminating in this latest design 'speed cuffs', issued in 1994

MOBILE SUPPORT UNITS

Inevitably, over the course of the Force history, Detective Sergeant Robert Kidd has not been the only officer to be attacked on duty. There have been many. One particular incident is notable for the singular courage of the officer concerned. It occurred on a dark night in 1955 when PC Don Norton and two colleagues surprised a gang of wagon thieves in Carlton Loop Sidings, Newark. The officers were immediately set upon in what erupted into a vicious and desperate struggle. One of the officers was left unconscious, another was dazed, while PC Norton was attacked with a rope tied to a steel hook which became embedded in his skull. He was spun around by another attacker and struck again on the head, this time with his own truncheon. Despite his desperate state, he made his way to a police station, more than a mile away, still with the hook in his skull and trailing the rope. He was rushed to hospital for immediate surgery. A massive search involving four police forces led eventually to the arrest of four well known criminals, one of whom was sentenced to 14 years, the others to eight years each. It transpired that one of those arrested, Leonard Mangham, had previously escaped justice when he lay in wait for a British Transport Commission police dog that had been released to apprehend him. Armed with a lead loaded stick, he had attacked the dog and rendered it unconscious. PC Don Norton had certainly cheated death in the sidings, and along with both his colleagues, he received the Queen's Commendation For Bravery. He subsequently returned to duty though he never fully recovered from the injuries he received that night.

In May 1980 the Home Office hosted a Working Conference on Violence on Public Transport, chaired jointly by the Home Secretary and the Minister of Transport. Their findings revealed that so far that year, no less than 320 incidents of assault had been carried out on BTP officers in the workplace. Among the results of the Conference was the recruitment of 100 extra officers for London Underground, and the establishment of Divisional Mobile Support Units, each of which comprised five Constables, one Sergeant, and one Inspector in overall command. Together they worked hard to reduce incidents of late night violence, vandalism and football hooliganism.

The Mobile Support Unit vehicle.

Unfortunately, some isolated incidents of assault on officers continue. In the early morning of 26th October 1985 PC Neil Harvey was found slumped over the loading bay of a warehouse in Castle Meadow Road, Nottingham. He was barely conscious and had been badly beaten, his face swollen to twice its normal size with multiple fractures, including a fractured skull. A heavy trail of blood wove haphazardly for over 300 feet back and fore across the road, tracing his agonised path. PC

Harvey spent the next seven days sedated and unconscious on a life support machine at the Queens Medical Centre. He recovered slowly but his face and the sight in his right eye remained permanently impaired and he never again returned to police duties. About the time Neil Harvey regained consciousness, four local youths were arrested, two of whom were already on bail for assaulting WPC Linda Brown. Charged with attempted murder, all four were subsequently convicted of assault with intent to cause grievous bodily harm and sentenced to eight years custody.

CRIMINAL PROCEDURE REFORMS

The 1984 Police and Criminal Evidence Act, relating to custody duties, produced the biggest single procedural change the police service had ever had placed upon it. The Act became operative in January 1986, with police stations classified 'designated' or 'non-designated'. Designated stations could detain prisoners for extended periods, whilst 'non-designated' could detain them for a maximum of six hours. The Act also saw the appointment of official Custody Officers, who remained outside case involvement and therefore ensured 'fair play'. In 1995 all BTP stations remain non-designated; however, several stations are empowered to charge and bail prisoners. The Act does not apply in Scotland, where prisoners are charged and processed in a self-contained police station in Glasgow. Other features of the Act included a revised complaints and discipline procedure, and community consultative bodies, set up by Chief Constables to ensure liaison between staff and the public.

The Prosecution of Offences Act of 1985 also became operative in 1986, whereby an independent Crown Prosecution Service was formed to take over the role of prosecutor from all police forces. Essentially, police officers are now investigators and witnesses within the judicial process, whilst the Crown Prosecution Service provides advocates to conduct the majority of prosecutions, irrespective of the gravity of the offence.

CLOSED CIRCUIT TELEVISION

In 1985 vandals set light to a stationary Intercity train at Polmadie Railway Depot in Scotland, creating over half a million pounds worth of damage. The culprits were later arrested; but this incident and others highlighted a need for much tighter security. In response to the problem, Closed Circuit Television, pioneered in Euston and Victoria stations, was introduced in selected vulnerable areas. CCTV proved itself to be an extremely cost effective means of preventing and detecting crime. Linked to the control room at the Area Headquarters and financed by the rail companies, it was an excellent example of how the BTP crime prevention officers and the rail companies could work together to the benefit of the railways. Such was its success that CCTV is now widely used by Forces all over the world.

The new control room at Area Headquarters in Glasgow.

High profile policing in London's Underground.

A notable example of CCTV's application may be seen in the London Underground where, it has been suggested, fear of violence poses far greater problems than violence itself. In 1989 only 12% of the 15,893 offences on London Underground involved violence; the rest consisted of petty theft. Nevertheless, fear has kept many people away, and the potential financial loss is considerable. In response to the problem, three pilot schemes were introduced during the late '80s and early '90s. The first of these was implemented on the Northern Line and, as well as the installation of CCTV, introduced assistance points with information and emergency handles, and improved lighting schemes. The number of robberies fell from 82 in 1986 to 8 in 1989. Similar schemes were implemented at Oxford Circus and at stations between Leytonstone and Barking. In addition, in 1988 a four million pound control room was opened at 'L' Division's headquarters at Broadway,

with display screens, computers and high-tech radio communications
that allow operators to monitor stations 24 hours a day, assess trouble
spots and dispatch officers in the minimum of time. These schemes
have now been extended to other areas of the Division.

COMPUTER TECHNOLOGY

Since 6th December 1986 BTP has had full access to the Police
National Computer, so that all communications between the Force and
the National Identification Bureau (the central registry located at New
Scotland Yard of crimes and criminals, now called the National
Identification Service) are direct rather than channelled through local
Home Office Forces.

*Monitoring public
order at Notting Hill
Carnival, 1995.*

Other computer systems installed include the Police National Legal
Database, run by a consortium of Forces, and Map Master, which
involves the electronic display of over 200,000 visual images of
ordnance survey maps which are stored on video discs and overlaid

with locations of police and ambulance stations. The system is invaluable, not least when the need arises to liaise with local police forces and emergency services, or when officers must be quickly dispatched to scenes of crime or disasters.

Computer technology aids the Force in many ways, increasing effectiveness and response times.

THE CID INDUCTION COURSE

During 1994 two officers of the British Transport Police, Detective Inspector Alan Wilson and Detective Sergeant John Neal, piloted a two-week induction course to the CID at Tadworth. The course was unique in that it was totally practical and skill-based. Previously, officers had been selected on the basis of written application and interview. The new course presents potential CID officers with a crime investigation scenario; they then work as a team to solve the 'mystery', with mock TV and Press appeals, and meetings with witnesses and informants. It has now become the model CID course for all Forces across the country.

TWO MASS MURDER CASES

It was during the 1980s that the British Transport Police, working in conjunction with Home Office Forces, were involved with their two biggest murder cases. The first case began to gain momentum in August 1983 when Keiran Patrick Kelly, a violent-tempered Irish vagrant strangled fellow vagrant William Boyd with a garrotte improvised from his socks and shoelaces, in a police cell at Clapham Station. Kelly was well known to officers of the British Transport Police: he tended to hang around the City stations, and in addition to receiving some 41 convictions for drink-related offences, had previously been tried and acquitted for the murder of one vagrant and the attempted murder of another, whom he had pushed in front of a tube train – miraculously the man had fallen through a gap in the rails and escaped with barely a scratch. Kelly later admitted to Detective Inspector John Hennigan of the BTP that he had killed at least nine other 'winos' in this way over a 30-year period, and many others besides. This astonishing and horrific allegation would make him one of the country's most prolific murderers; however, with Kelly knowing his victims only by their street names, evidence was almost impossible to come by and the allegation was never proven.

When Kelly came to trial for the murder of Boyd, a consultant psychiatrist explained how Kelly loathed his fellow vagrants, despite living among them, and described him as 'incorrigible in penal terms and incurable in medical terms'. The Judge agreed. Police were satisfied he had killed at least five times and in 1984 he was ultimately tried for the murder of Hector Fisher, a retired printer who had befriended him, for which he received a life sentence. He was subsequently tried and found guilty of the manslaughter of William Boyd, and received a further life sentence.

The second case was opened on 6th April 1986 when two children found 26-year-old Anthony Connolly strangled and horribly mutilated in a plate-layer's cabin beside the railway in Brixton. The victim was known to be a homosexual who frequented London's gay clubs and pubs, and in the pursuance of leads, undercover officers set about trawling them for evidence. The breakthrough occurred when the Kensington branch of the Metropolitan referred a BR worker over to BTP Detective Chief Inspector David Furness at Stockwell, who reported to Furness how a man he had met in a gay public house had tried to strangle him that same evening in a South London lorry park. The Metropolitan Murder Squad had meanwhile been investigating the murder of 37-year-old James Burns, also a homosexual, and found similarly strangled and mutilated in a derelict basement flat in Kensington early in March of that year. Furness made a connection between the three incidents and the hunt was on for a serial killer.

On 15th May plain clothes BTP officers, in radio contact with others near-by, accompanied the BR worker to a number of gay pubs and clubs, hoping to spot his attacker. A few hours later, at the Prince of Wales public house, Michael Lupo, an Italian living and working in London, was identified. He was arrested and led outside, remaining calm, composed and co-operative throughout.

Detective Chief Inspector Furness and Detective Inspector Ellcock from the Metropolitan Police led a series of interviews with Lupo, who not only admitted to the murder of Connolly and Burns, but to two others. The first was that of an unidentified tramp on Hungerford Bridge near Charing Cross Railway Station, who had made the mistake of asking Lupo for a light for his cigarette; the murder was already being investigated by Detective Inspector Jim Walton. The second had not yet been reported. Officers were dispatched to a basement flat in Earls Court, the location given by Lupo and, sure enough, there made the gruesome discovery of hospital worker Damien McCluskey.

Lupo's history was to be unfolded over the next few weeks. Following a strict Catholic upbringing he had served in the Italian Army, but having realised his sexuality, had deserted and moved to London. He worked successfully in the fashion and beauty industry, charming the celebrities and distinguished acquaintances he surrounded himself with; hiding from them his other life, in which he cruised the gay clubs and pubs of London to satisfy an insatiable sexual appetite. He alleged to have had between four and five thousand partners in a year, his sexual tastes becoming increasingly sadomasochistic until he had become impotent and, during an eight-week period, resorted to murder and mutilation. He was described as 'a psychopath'.

On 10th July 1987 Lupo received four life sentences, with seven years to run consecutively for the two attempted murders. During the sentencing, Sir James Miskin, Recorder of London, talked of the 'appalling background' to the case, commenting on the courage of the BR worker who had identified his attacker, and praising the police for their performance. The gay circles in London were often suspicious and hostile towards the police and DCI Furness paid tribute to his men who had worked in 'harrowing and difficult' circumstances.

Lupo died in prison of an AIDS-related illness in 1995.

Chapter Fourteen

MAJOR INCIDENTS

MOORGATE RAIL CRASH

On 28th February 1975, Britain suffered its worst ever Underground disaster – Leslie Newson, the driver of a train travelling from Drayton Park, simply failed to stop at Moorgate Station, his train ploughing through the buffers at 40 miles an hour and finishing up in a head-on collision with the tunnel wall. Forty-two people were left dead, 82 seriously injured and many other passengers and rescue workers traumatised for years to come.

Detective Constable Jim Crowe had been dealing with an offender at Lambeth when a message came through of the incident at Moorgate. He and his colleagues set off immediately for the station. They searched the top station first and found nothing amiss; so they turned their attention downstairs, where 40 or so passengers travelling at the rear of the train had already alighted – they were aware of little more than a heavy bump and a few broken windows. The platform lights were on but the train itself was in darkness. The officers phoned headquarters to report what they had seen, and returned to the train. Only then did the horrendous picture begin to unfold – that the front three coaches had in fact been squashed into the space of one.

In the confined space, darkness and immense heat, conditions for the police and rescue workers were horrific. Bodies were decomposing quickly, and officers had to wear boiler suits and wellington boots and walk through a disinfectant trough before leaving and entering the scene. Twenty years after the incident, the terrible smell of rotting flesh is what most officers recall first. A huge fan was set up to blow cool air into the tunnel, and firemen soon found they had to use hand cutting equipment as the oxycetelin equipment was using up valuable oxygen.

As each survivor was cut free of the wreckage, so they were stretchered up to the fleet of awaiting ambulances. DC Deacon recalled that every time they appeared with a casualty at the exit barriers, they were blinded by a sea of flash bulbs from the world's press.

BTP officers assisting casualties at Moorgate.

Soup kitchens were set up for the mass of workers, fire crew, ambulance staff, and doctors and nurses from Guy's and Bart's hospitals. Over the next few days, passengers' property had to be recovered to help identify some of the victims. It was a massive operation. Due to the health risks, officers were allowed to work around the scene for only 20 minutes of every hour for a week. It was some five days before the last body – that of the driver – was released from the wreckage.

PC Jock Blanchard with other emergency staff at Moorgate.
Courtesy of the London Transport Museum

If anything good could be said to have come from the nightmare of Moorgate, it was the relationship that developed between the BTP and the City of London Police who worked so closely in those difficult circumstances.

THE POLMONT DISASTER

Scotland has seen its fair share of disasters on the railways. One of the most famous was the collapse of the Tay Bridge in 1879, bringing a train and its 75 passengers to their deaths in the icy waters of the river. Exactly one hundred years later, on 22nd October, a train from Glasgow ran into the rear of a train stopped by a faulty signal near Invergowrie Bay. The collision sent the coaches tumbling into the water and resulted in the deaths of five people, with many more injured. Inspector Colin Monro, at the time a young PC, was one of the first on the scene of the accident – the first he had attended. The image of the rescue services struggling to free the passengers from the train remains with him, in particular the steam cranes lifting a carriage from the water and a lifeless body being hauled out from the mud underneath it and into a waiting dinghy. This grim scene is one to which many officers attending Major Incidents can relate.

The Invergowrie Crash. The coaches were eventually moved and now lie buried beneath part of the landfall site by the River Tay.
Courtesy of Science & Society Picture Library

The Forth Bridge – part of the Scottish Area's beat.

One of the more recent rail crashes to involve the Scottish Division was the 1984 Polmont Disaster. On 31st July a packed Edinburgh to Glasgow commuter train hit a bullock that had strayed onto the line. The train was derailed, resulting in 13 dead and 44 injured. Assistant Chief Constable MacKenzie was travelling in a carriage that turned 180 degrees before demolishing a stone perimeter wall and finally embedding itself in the penultimate carriage. MacKenzie recalls the violent deceleration of the train before a terrific impact; then everything fell strangely quiet and calm. Realising that he was only bruised and shaken, his BTP training enabled him to take control of himself and the situation as he set about making a reconnaissance of the damage. He was joined by a young, newly qualified woman doctor, dressed, poignantly, in a flowing, white summer dress, and together they began establishing the location of the dead and administering help to the injured and other passengers before the emergency crews arrived. The young doctor was to learn a great deal very quickly about the nature of crash victims.

The Polmont
derailing.

THE MINERS STRIKE

British Transport Police were naturally involved in many aspects of the 1984 Miners' Strike, primarily in the control of pickets at locomotive depots and rail heads adjacent to pit heads, so that lines were kept open for the essential supply of coal to power stations. Tensions ran particularly high in the Nottinghamshire and Derbyshire areas where train-drivers, signalmen and guards were moving coal for the ASLEF men from Shirebrook Colliery who had opted to work, despite their Union's instructions, necessitating a near-constant attendance by the Leeds Mobile Support Unit. It was not only picketers who caused problems: during the Strike many people took to digging coal from the railway embankments, resulting in subsidence collapsing onto the passing trains. Tragically, two children from Leeds were killed in this way. Stone-throwing and arson also caused damage, mostly to train bodies and signal equipment, and nation-wide some 460 arrests were made. On the whole, good relations were maintained between British Rail staff, local and visiting police forces, and with most of the picketers themselves. Not a single complaint was made about BTP officers' conduct.

The Miners Strike.
Courtesy of Science & Society Picture Library

THE KINGS CROSS FIRE

Twelve years after Moorgate, on the evening of 18th November 1987, a passenger travelling up the Piccadilly Line escalator noticed a small fire between the tread and the skirting board – the result of a cigarette dropped carelessly into an accumulation of grease, dust and debris below. A railwayman was alerted and two policemen, PC Bebbington and PC Kerbey of BTP, were called in; they in turn called the fire brigade and arranged for all three escalators to be closed. However, in growing panic, passengers pushed past two railwaymen, removed the restrictive tape and continued to use one of the escalators.

Piccadilly and Victoria Line trains were ordered not to stop and an evacuation was put into operation. By the time the first of the fire crews arrived at 7.42, 10 minutes after being called, flames in the escalator shaft were between five and six feet high and Station Officer Colin Townsley ordered his men to put on breathing apparatus. Tragically, Colin Townsley was one of the 31 people to die that night.

The decision was made to evacuate passengers on and around the Victoria Line platform. This meant their exiting through the ticket hall, which moments later became an inferno, the result of a 'flash-over' in which dense, hot, acrid smoke burst from the throat of the escalator shaft into the ticket hall and out to the station exits, with temperatures exceeding 600°C. Many people caught fire, whilst others stumbled about in thick smoke trying to find exits or fought desperately to clamber onto moving trains whose drivers had been ordered not to stop at the station.

By coincidence, a number of BTP officers had been in the vicinity of Kings Cross awaiting another duty at Euston later in the evening. Some had begun to patrol the tube and main line stations and in doing so were among the first on the scene of the incident.

The Kings Cross Fire

Other officers having heard the emergency radio call to Force Headquarters raced to join them. By midnight 82 BTP officers were in attendance. The scale of the fire and its consequences will remain etched in the hearts and minds of all of them. Following the fire Constables Kenneth Kerbey, Graham Martland, Richard Kukielka, Patrick Balfe, Julian Dixon, Terry Bebbington and Steven Hanson (all of whom were badly injured), received awards for gallantry.

CLAPHAM RAIL CRASH

On 12th December 1988, the 07.18 from Basingstoke and the 06.14 from Poole, both full of commuters, headed as usual towards Clapham en route to Waterloo. In the opposite direction, the 08.03 to Haslemere was running, without passengers, towards the same cutting. On reaching Clapham, Mr McClymont, the driver of the Basingstoke train, spotted an incorrect signal and, in accordance with the Rule Book, stopped to report it. Turning from the line-side telephone installed for such purposes, he heard the impact as the Poole train crashed head-on into the back of his own train, and saw it pushed some ten feet forwards. The Poole train driver had approached the cutting through signals in his favour and, having cleared a 'blind' left hand curve, must have felt his heart stop as his worst nightmare confronted him – a stationary train with no stopping distance. The force of the collision knocked his train off side, and as the Haslemere train approached seconds later, its second carriage collided with the Poole train. The impact of the front of the Poole train on the last carriage of the Basingstoke train had caused it to be thrown up above the ten-foot concrete wall at the side of the cutting. It finally came to rest on the embankment above the wall, with several other coaches derailed. A further Waterloo-bound train was at this moment approaching the scene, totally oblivious of the carnage in front of it. Mercifully, driver Barry Pike saw it in time and was able to stop with just 60 yards to spare between his own train and the rear of the one from Poole.

British Transport Police Inspector Michael Foster had been travelling that morning in the fifth carriage of the Basingstoke train. Immediately after the collision he pulled on a high visibility jacket and jumped down onto the tracks to assess the situation. He then telephoned the signal box to alert the emergency services to 'a major accident'. Inspector Foster had a good working knowledge of the railways, not only because of his transport police training, but because prior to joining the Force in 1969 he had been a locomotive fireman, and because he knew the driver of his train personally. All this enabled him to respond to the situation very quickly; but even so, he maintains that it was not until the early hours of the following morning that the extent of what he had been involved in really hit him. He described the deathly 'hush' that hung in the air the first few minutes after impact, with everyone remaining exactly where they had landed until rail staff, emergency services and other members of BTP arrived to help them out. They were the lucky ones. Thirty-five train crew and passengers had been killed, all having travelled in the first two coaches of the Poole train which had had its left side completely ripped open. The first third of the leading coach, carrying driver John Rolls, had disintegrated completely.

PURLEY RAIL CRASH

On 4th March 1989, only four months after the Clapham crash, and whilst the investigation was still under way, another major accident occurred, this time at Purley in Surrey. The 12.50 Horsham to Victoria train, travelling behind time, was crossing from the Up slow line to the Up fast line at Purley when the 12.17 Littlehampton to Victoria train failed to stop at a red signal, and came crashing into it at around 55 miles per hour. The Littlehampton train then plunged down a steep embankment and landed close to some houses. Media headlines of 'It's another Clapham' sent chills down people's spines.

Superintendent Martin Taylor, who was involved in the subsequent investigation, described how access to the steep embankment became increasingly muddy and difficult for the rescue workers, and how a garage of one of the near-by houses had to be knocked down to facilitate access. Branches of the crushed trees had pierced the trains carriages, hampering the recovery still further, but all the passengers, including the five dead and 87 injured, were removed from the scene within an hour and 45 minutes.

The driver's failure to stop was to earn him a charge of manslaughter; whilst the two accidents, Clapham and then Purley, combined to raise fears about the safety of train travel to unprecedented levels. Superintendent Taylor remains in personal contact with many of the victims and families of those lost in the crash, and lends his support at annual memorial services.

Purley rail crash. The trees combined with the steep embankment made rescue work difficult. Here it can be clearly seen that the fire brigade are given priority in the rescue, whilst BTP officers co-ordinate the operation and investigate the cause.

The official report on the Clapham Crash notes the co-operation between the emergency services as 'excellent'; and to ensure that this would remain so, recommended that major incident training should take place on a regular basis, financed by British Rail, facilitated by the British Transport Police, and involving all of the emergency services. Area Moderators were appointed to co-ordinate these 'table-top' exercises, and during 1994/95, 135 were run, along with eight 'live' exercises. In addition to these measures, the Association of Chief Police Officers (ACPO) now publish National Contingency Planning guide-lines and the BTP produce comprehensive Incident Planning manuals.

BTP officers working alongside fire and ambulance crews to rescue victims of the 1991 Severn Tunnel Crash. 185 passengers were injured when a Portsmouth to Cardiff sprinter train ran into the rear of a Paddington to Cardiff Intercity train inside the Severn Tunnel.

Courtesy of South West News Service

Mobile Incident Vehicles.

Chapter Fifteen

FOOTBALL HOOLIGANISM

THE BTP FOOTBALL UNIT

With 122 professional football clubs in Britain today, there is fairly constant movement of fans around the UK and overseas; and throughout the nine-month season their behaviour is a matter of increasing concern for the general public, the transport industry, and the Police Forces whose responsibility it is to control them. The size of the crowd, the excitement of the match and rivalry between team supporters, so often intensified by alcohol – all combine to create volatile situations which are, at the very least, intimidating, and at worst, life-threatening.

Since the early 1970s, the British Transport Police has become increasingly involved with efforts to control the problem, and a number of constructive steps have been taken, starting in 1973 when it became routine procedure to police all fan-carrying trains. Annual matches between England and Scotland, held alternately at Wembley and Hampden Park, were particularly notorious, although the differences in police law meant that 50 or so English officers had to be in Scotland two days before a match in order to be sworn in as Constables for that area – inevitably becoming a strain on the Force in economic terms as well as in man-power considerations.

The leading coach of a Luton to Euston train was completely gutted by fire started by Chelsea fans (1975).

With fights breaking out between rival fans crossing the Channel for European matches in 1983 and 1984, BTP officers also began accompanying them on ferries. The disturbances resulted in a working party on football violence, chaired by the Department of the Environment where it was acknowledged that an official central intelligence unit was required. It was also acknowledged that, in view of the invaluable information the BTP could provide, they were the Force to provide it.

The result was the formation of the BTP Football Unit, headed by Inspector Dennis Temporal and aided by PC Andy Douglas. The primary role of the Football Unit was to obtain and disseminate intelligence throughout BTP and other Forces and agencies who had an interest in the whereabouts and activities of supporters. For example, if trains of rival fans were to stop for signals in the same location, all hell could break loose, with windows smashed and trains trashed. The Unit therefore collated all of the available information, arranged meetings to share plans and de-briefings with associated parties, telexed the various bodies with up-to-date information and, where required, mobilised BTP officers to deal with potential problems. In addition, Mobile Support Units were organised to tail fans – Leeds gang members nicknamed the North East Division Unit 'grasshoppers' as they never knew where or when they were going to turn up next – and under-cover surveillance officers mixed with, and worked at being accepted by gangs as one of their own. In this way the Unit gained invaluable details of fights, drug dealings and robberies, including the practice of 'steaming', in which large gangs steam through crowds lifting such items as purses, bags and jewellery.

Interestingly, the Unit's work revealed that not all offenders could be stereo-typed as 'young thugs': for example, a number of company directors, solicitors and other 'respected' professionals were found to be using matches as a front, behind which they organised drug deals and other major criminal activities.

As the Unit became established, excellent relationships developed between the British Transport and Home Office Forces, the Dutch Marechausée, the Belgian Gendarmerie, the French Police de l'Air et des Frontières, and other national Police Forces located where European matches were taking place. Officers work hard to develop good relations with the supporters too. Their success may be measured by such gestures as the one following the Kings Cross fire, when football fans made a collection between them and requested that it be donated to an injured BTP officer. Good behaviour is reported back to Clubs as promptly as the bad.

The presence of police dogs helps to minimise public order offences.

THE HEYSEL STADIUM DISASTER

More often than not, alcohol is the root cause behind rampaging football fans. On 29th May 1985 its effect was tragically demonstrated at Brussels' Heysel Stadium where thousands of fans gathered to watch Liverpool play Juventus in a European Cup Final they would never forget.

The European Cup Winners Cup Final had been played only a few days earlier on 15th May. Around 16,000 Everton fans had travelled successfully to and from the Merseyside area to watch the match, with intelligence dispatched from BTP HQ and used extensively throughout Holland. The date for the Cup Final set, contact was immediately made with Liverpool Football Club where enquiries yielded information that some 8,000 fans would be travelling to Brussels in arranged groups. 5,900 of the fans were to travel by air and coach, whilst 2,100 were to travel on BR sponsored trains, escorted by BTP. Although isolated incidents of unruly behaviour had occurred in the past, Liverpool fans were generally regarded to be well behaved and trouble was not anticipated.

On 23rd May a meeting was held at Tadworth, attended by representatives of the Belgian Gendarmerie, PAF Calais, Calais Town Police, Dutch Marechausée, Dutch Railway Police, Kent Constabulary, Dover and Harbour Board Police, British Transport Police, the Department of Environment (Sports) and the Department of Transport. The meeting de-briefed the Everton fixture and discussed arrangements for the Liverpool game. At the request of the Chief of Brussels City Police, BTP were to send eight Liverpool-based officials to Brussels. Initially they were to police trains from Liverpool in uniform, but on entering Belgium or boarding Belgian ships their jurisdiction would cease and they would act instead as liaison officers. In addition, a large body of fully-briefed senior stewards from Liverpool Football Club and the Merseyside Police Football Liaison Inspector were to travel with fans.

The outward journey was relatively uneventful. Under Byelaw 3 (A) of the British Railways Board of September 1980, all alcohol had to be surrendered before embarking on designated trains; and whilst some fans had already been drinking and were in boisterous, noisy mood, all were judged fit to travel. Ships were also 'dry' and supporters were well behaved. Between 10.00 a.m. and 2.00 p.m. trains arrived at the station serving the stadium, which itself was heavily policed with officers from 19 independent Forces in Brussels. BTP officers were taken to the Special Operations room at Brussels City Police HQ, from where key points were being observed by CCTV.

It was in Brussels that the problem began, as alcohol could now be sold freely, literally by the caseload, and temperatures and emotions were beginning to rise. Due to minor problems with fans, BTP liaison officers were requested to accompany the mobile patrols in various areas of the city. Around 2.30 p.m. some 2,000 Liverpool supporters took over the Grande Plasse, singing, dancing, drinking heavily, their ring leaders gathered on the bandstand ignoring the Belgian Police requests to disperse. Assistant Chief Constable Ian McGregor courageously went onto the bandstand himself, whereupon the fans obeyed his order to move out. Later in the day, officers noticed other groups of Liverpool fans drinking heavily around the town. The atmosphere was becoming increasingly tense.

By 6.30 p.m. 400 police officers had assembled inside the stadium, and 400 outside. Heavily armed members of the para-military riot police, the fire brigade and a number of medical teams were also present. By 7.00 p.m. the mood was switching from tense to ugly. In the Liverpool end of the stand, supporters were beginning to respond to the antagonisms of Juventus supporters. There were a number of surges towards the dividing wire by both sides; and eventually the Liverpool fans charged at their rivals. In the ensuing retreat by the Juventus fans, a wall collapsed and 39 Italians were crushed to death.

Meanwhile, ACC McGregor had been making a rendezvous just outside with his officers regarding post-match tactics. He could hear chanting and screams from within the stadium and saw a number of people running towards him in great distress. McGregor and his officers immediately re-entered the stadium to find 'total pandemonium' had broken out. People were running around screaming, others were injured and some were obviously dead.

Heysel was a tragedy that had simply burst out of control: partly the result of alcohol – under the circumstances at the time, impossible to ban – and partly, it was discovered, the result of a poorly maintained stadium. Certainly police officers did everything in their power to limit the damage and destruction. As the dead and injured were carried from the scene of the disaster, ACC McGregor liaised with numerous officials of the British Consulate and Belgian Railway Police to arrange immediate transport of supporters back to Ostend. Together with Liverpool Stewards and BR Officials, BTP officers supervised the loading of over 3,000 supporters onto trains back to Ostend and then to Dover. Everyone was stunned and the mood was one of total submission. The presence of BTP officers throughout was reported as 'invaluable' to both Belgian authorities and the British supporters, with whom they became a reassuring feature.

As a result of the Government reports following the disaster, the British Transport Police were given full access to the Police National Computer, providing a central store of information hitherto available to Home Office Forces only. The Force became 'live' on the Police National Computer in December 1986, marking another milestone in its history.

Despite problems, good relations between officers and supporters are encouraged.

KONINGEN BEATRIX

On 7th August 1986 another major incident, this time en route to a match, was to further damage the reputation of UK football supporters. On this occasion, pre-season international 'friendly' matches were being played in Germany and Holland and a group of around 150 fans from a variety of clubs set out from Harwich to the Hook of Holland. The scheduled crossing was carrying around 2,000 passengers in all.

Only an hour after departure, a fight broke out in a bar between a group of Manchester United fans and some lorry drivers. The bar was closed for a short time whilst order was restored but when it reopened, trouble flared straight up again, with fans singing, chanting, and generally intimidating other passengers. A small band stopped performing and left the bar, whereupon one fan took control of the abandoned microphone and continued to incite the others. A large group went in search of rival West Ham supporters, who were holed up in another bar, and on meeting them, fierce fighting broke out. The stairs on which they fought were described in later reports as being 'awash with blood'. Glass display cabinets were smashed and pieces of glass used as weapons, along with hoses, fire extinguishers and knives. The fighting continued for some 45 minutes, creating over £20,000 worth of damage to the vessel. Captain Nagel took the decision to return the ship to Harwich and radioed ahead to the British Transport Police at Parkeston Quay.

As the ship came in at 3.30 a.m., BTP officers and officers from the Essex Force were waiting to remove the troublesome supporters. Of the 75 that were removed, 14 were positively identified and accordingly arrested.

On board the Koningin Beatrix.

Detective Inspector Mick Barry and a team of ten detective officers headed the subsequent enquiry, based at the Kings Cross, BTP station, and the trial at Chelmsford Crown Court in December 1987 led to nine offenders being found guilty. They received sentences ranging between one and eight years' imprisonment.

THE NATIONAL FOOTBALL INTELLIGENCE UNIT

Following the Heysel Stadium, Koningin Beatrix and other high profile incidents, the Government took a number of serious measures aimed at containing hooliganism. One of these was an extension of the ban on the sale of alcohol to fan-carrying buses, coaches and at stadiums, which has resulted in a major improvement in behaviour, although some fans have been found concealing alcohol in soft drinks bottles and cartons, and even injected into oranges. Another measure is the introduction of club membership schemes.

Most significantly, in 1989 the National Football Intelligence Unit (NFIU) was created to deal specifically with international football relations. PC Andy Douglas was seconded as the British Transport Police representative, with Dennis Temporal remaining as the Force Football Liaison Officer until his retirement in 1992 – two years earlier his services had been rewarded with an MBE.

Dennis Temporal, MBE.

The NFIU comprises officers from several Forces, based at Spring Gardens in Central London. Their computer database stores such data as gang member details, as well as images transferred from video footage taken inside the football grounds. Following the introduction of these measures, incidents of violence have dropped dramatically; although large scale organised crime, incidents of general skirmishes and public disorder remain a problem. The NFIU is now a part of the National Criminal Intelligence Service (NCIS).

Work continues. Prior to the 1990 World Cup in Italy, 50 Italian police officers, selected from their own Forces, were sent to Britain to prepare for the arrival in their home country of English fans. In addition, Andy Douglas travelled to Rome for the five weeks the England team was present, liaising with the town and city commanders.

A group of Italian Carabineri Officers seconded to the BTP, together with Chief Constable Desmond O'Brien, Inspector Dennis Temporal and other senior officers.

As Euro '96 Cup Championships draw closer, plans are well in hand for the policing of the many thousands of European fans who will travel around the country and through the Channel Tunnel direct to Manchester and other well-known football cities.

Chapter Sixteen

TERRORISM

Following the seemingly endless series of disasters that struck the railways during the 1980s, the 1990s saw another threat to public safety on Britain's railways reach unprecedented levels – terrorism. The explosion that rocked Paddington Station at 4 a.m. on 18th February 1991 was to signal the start of a three and a half year bombing campaign that targeted the whole nation's railway network.

The vulnerability of railway stations had first been exploited in February 1884 when a bomb exploded in a Victoria Station cloakroom, killing an army officer and injuring several civilians. All London stations were subsequently searched and the following day three more devices found, each consisting of a clock and several pounds of dynamite. The bombs were thought to be the work of the Fenians, forerunners of the Irish Republican Army.

Terrorism flared up again on 26th July 1939 when the Irish demand for the withdrawal of English troops from Northern Ireland made itself heard loud and clear with a bomb explosion in the left-luggage office at King's Cross Station. A young Scotsman was killed, and his wife and 14 other people injured. Sadly this was only the first of a spate of attacks, which continued through the war years, much to the horror of the Government whose efforts were concentrated on the threat of Hitler's invading armies. Railway Police took to searching any and all packages that were to be left, or had already been abandoned, in stations until they were satisfied they posed no threat.

The IRA campaign stepped up apace in the early 1970s, with bomb explosions at Kings Cross, Victoria, Euston and Sloane Square Stations. Though isolated, these incidents were serious, and large numbers of officers were subsequently deployed to act both as a deterrent and a reassurance to the public. In addition closer links were forged with anti-terrorist squads and bomb disposal officers.

On 21st November 1974 IRA bombs exploded in two Birmingham pubs, killing 21 young people and injuring many more. The incident was to create the greatest bomb outrage in the history of the country. On the evening of the explosion, several BTP officers were attending a promotion examination lecture at New Street Station Police Office only 100 yards away from the Mulberry Bush bar on the ground floor of the Rotunda, and therefore were among the first to witness the carnage there. New Street Police Office became a forward incident post in the early stages of the emergency. Enquiries by New Street CID officers, with the help of an alert booking clerk, led to the arrest by BTP officers of six suspects who had travelled by train from Birmingham to Heysham, where they were boarding the ferry for Ireland. The six were subsequently found guilty of the murders but served only 16 years before having their convictions overturned amid much controversy and public attention in 1991. Following their release, the West Midlands Police conducted another lengthy enquiry to review the evidence from 1974, at which considerable assistance was once again sought and given by serving and retired members of the BTP. No public acknowledgement has ever been made of the part played by the British Transport Police in the affair.

The Birmingham bombing was not the last major incident of the 1970s. At 8.48 a.m. on 4th March 1976 an explosion ripped open the roof of a train as it left Cannon Street Station. Passengers on a passing train were injured by flying glass but fortunately the train itself was empty. A massive investigation began, with regular appeals over the station loud speakers for travellers who might have knowledge of the perpetrators.

Bomb explosion at London's Cannon Street Station.

Only 11 days later another incident took place. On this occasion a terrorist carried the bomb in a briefcase with him onto a train at West Ham Station, presumably intending to leave it behind him when he alighted; but smoke began filtering out from the case and in alarm he threw it down the aisle where it exploded. Though himself injured by the blast, the terrorist attempted to escape, in the process shooting dead a railwayman who tried to stop him. He injured another passenger before being cornered by three policemen and shooting himself. Other incidents followed shortly, resulting in BTP officers conducting a massive search of every railway arch and lock-up on the network for evidence of some sort of bomb-making factory.

Railways were not the only target for terrorist bombs; the vast majority were military and government establishments, although the media interest and public shock factor gained from these was low in comparison. Certainly military establishments were the trend when the bomb exploded, without warning, at Paddington that Monday morning in 1991.

Within an hour of the explosion, police had received 20 'warnings' of further bombs – and they were only the first of 5,228 calls to be received during the whole campaign. Four hours after the Paddington incident, an explosion at Victoria left one man dead and 54 other people injured. And one week later a bomb exploded at St Albans, inflicting damage to the line but no human injuries.

'Warning' calls stretched police and railway resources to the limit. With every half-day closure of the network costing over £40 million in direct losses alone (indirect losses could be multiplied 100-fold), it was obvious that stations could not be closed automatically when a call was received. The chances of a warning being genuine were low; but it was vital to treat each one seriously and to assess it individually. Preservation of life was the primary concern, and every practical precaution had to be taken.

Victoria Station after an explosion.

Having previously served in the Royal Ulster Constabulary, Chief Constable Desmond O'Brien had considerable experience in dealing with terrorism, as had former Army Bomb Squad Officer Adrian Dwyer who was brought in as Force Search Advisor. By the third Monday of the campaign the crisis was being managed and a strategic response formulated. New security measures included the removal of litter bins from station concourses, the installation of Closed Circuit TV cameras in strategic positions and the briefing of all railway staff, from toilet cleaners to executives.

Over the course of the campaign a change was seen in the trend of the bombers. During 1991 Central London stations were targeted. By '92 security measures had become more effective and attacks were being targeted at the track. 1993 saw the bombers moving their targets to stations outside London. And by 1994 bombs were being found outside the stations, in car parks, on the street and on the railway lines. Media attention – the life blood of any terrorist organisation – was lessening, and eventually, with the cease-fire of August, the campaign ended. One person had been killed and 83 injured on or near railway property.

THE HOME OFFICE LARGE MAJOR ENQUIRY SYSTEM (HOLMES)

Hoax telephone calls have always been a major problem for the police department. During the IRA campaign, some hoax callers used code words, others did not; some genuine calls used code words, others did not; genuine threats gave only short notice of an explosion. The time it takes to assess each call can be costly – and dangerous.

Using valuable experience gained when serving with the Essex Constabulary, Detective Chief Superintendent Peter Whent adapted the powerful computer system HOLMES to BTP use. It proved a major success, helping to make high risk management decisions based on reasoned judgement, and has set the standard for bomb threat analysis throughout the world.

An officer x-rays a suspicious article.

THE FORCE INTELLIGENCE BUREAU

The Force Intelligence Bureau, manned by selected CID officers, is the top level intelligence unit within the Force, its task to collate information to and from Home Office forces, Government and other agencies.

The 1990s bombing campaign covered a wide expanse of the country, but centred almost exclusively around the railways. Whilst Home Office county forces dealt with one or maybe two bombs each during the whole campaign, the BTP as Britain's only national Force dealt with 38 incidents of terrorism and 7,310 incidents of suspected terrorism. As a result of this, a Force Intelligence Bureau officer was permanently seconded to the Anti-Terrorist branch at New Scotland Yard. BTP is the only Force to have such representation.

POLICE SEARCH ADVISORS (POLSAS)

POLSAs are officers licensed to search for explosives, improvised explosive devices, fire arms, ammunition and documents. They advise how a search should proceed, train search teams (among them Bomb Car officers) and develop search awareness amongst all officers. Themselves trained by a joint military and Home Office team, POLSAs receive regular in-Force continuation training and Home Office refresher courses, and must be re-licensed every two years.

THE BOMB CAR

As part of the response to the terrorist campaign, a fully equipped 'Bomb Car' was brought into use in 1991 and remains on constant stand-by to deal with suspicious packages left on, or around, railway property. If a call is received, or a suspicious article found, the surrounding area is evacuated and Bomb Car officers called in. On average, suspicious packages can be cleared within 12 minutes of the officers' arrival at the scene; but when a suspicious item cannot be discounted, or an actual bomb is discovered, bomb squad officers from either the Metropolitan Police or the Army are called to make the device safe. The Bomb Car also carries equipment to deal with such threats as chemical weaponry, whose deadliness was so dramatically demonstrated on a Tokyo tube during the spring of 1995.

Police Search Adviser Alan Couper and the Bomb Car.

THE FORCE SEARCH ADVISOR

Fear of terrorism is actually more of a problem to the railways than terrorist acts themselves. The public must feel safe and protected and a high profile stance must be taken even during times of cease fire. The decision-makers who plan the railway infrastructure need to know how and why it is vulnerable and what they can do to protect it. Assurance must be given to staff as well as to the public. The Force

Search Advisor's responsibility is

1.   To train all search teams and run search awareness courses for all staff.

2.   To ensure that BTP policies are effective and appropriate.

3.   To advise the railway industry.

Explosive and Incendiary Devices discovered on railway property between 1st January 1991 and 11th October 1994

Explosive Devices

Date		*Place*
18 February	1991	Paddington
18 February	1991	Victoria
25 February	1991	St Albans
16 December	1991	Clapham Junction
28 February	1992	London Bridge
01 March	1992	White Hart Lane
10 March	1992	Wandsworth Common
09 October	1992	Arnos Grove
21 October	1992	Silver Street
21 October	1992	Willesden Junction
09 December	1992	Woodside Park
22 December	1992	Hampstead
03 February	1993	Kent House
03 February	1993	South Kensington
24 October	1993	Reading
24 October	1993	Basingstoke
24 October	1993	Reading
26 October	1993	Dorton (Bucks)
14 December	1993	West Byfleet
16 December	1993	Brookwood

15 March	1994	Sevenoaks
21 March	1994	Orpington
06 June	1994	Sevenoaks
13 June	1994	Stevenage
21 July	1994	Reading
22 Aug	1994	Oxford Circus

Incendiary Devices

03 April	1991	Preston
29 August	1991	Hammersmith
23 December	1991	Ilford
23 December	1991	Harrow on the Hill
23 December	1991	Neasden
31 January	1992	London Road
03 February	1992	Neasden
07 February	1992	Barking
20 September	1992	Crewe
02 November	1992	Manchester Victoria
20 December	1993	Northfields
10 October	1994	Liverpool Street
11 October	1994	Victoria

Chapter Seventeen

THE
BRITISH TRANSPORT POLICE
IN THE 1990s

SAFETY AWARENESS

Engendering safety awareness in the community is a crucial part of the work of the British Transport Police. To drive the message home, specially trained liaison officers visit schools throughout the country, sometimes accompanied by a British Rail train driver, to talk to children about the dangers of playing near the railways. Visual scenarios are sometimes created by the use of train carriages and pieces of track.

Liaison officers talking to young schoolchildren.

As well as national projects, BTP officers in each division work closely with Railtrack on their own initiatives. In the North East division, for example, the '95 Safety Drive' tackles a fresh issue every month, ranging from trespassing and its consequences, to graffiti and level crossing abuse, all of which have the potential to cause injury or death. A Railsafe Trophy Day has also been established, with school children competing in an annual fun day which maintains rail safety as its theme, featuring a soccer match, celebrity visits and sideshows. Everyone receives a T-shirt bearing the logo 'Kick it – Don't Play on the Railways'.

*The Railsafe Trophy Day, June 1994.
Winners of the Tournament at Seaton
Carew School from Hartlepool with
Lynne Miller, aka WPC Cathy Marshall
of ITV's The Bill.*

*The Scottish initiative, 'Crucial
Crew', is a two week course held
throughout Scotland which brings ten-
to 12-year-olds together with members of
the regional Police Force, Regional Fire
Brigade, Scottish Ambulance
Association, Regional Roads
Department, HM Coastguard,
Environmental Health Department,
Scottish Power and Scottish Gas.
Through role play, the aim is to help
children learn social responsibility, cope
with dangerous situations and avoid
becoming the victims of crime. Up to
1,200 children attend the course.*

Obstructions on the railway lines create numerous problems: at the very least they cause delay and disruption to services; at worst they can derail a train and cause injury or death. During 1994 30,000 trespass and vandal offences were reported, resulting in such national operations as Operation Rhino, run during the spring of 1995, which highlight their danger to the public. It included surveys of boundary fencing to improve security, clearing of lineside waste, high profile policing at troublespots, covert surveillance, train and car patrols, offender profiling, school visits, increased contact with staff at depots and stations, and liaison with the Crown Prosecution Service and local police forces. Supported and partially funded by Railtrack, Operation Rhino was outstandingly successful, with almost all parts of the country doubling their detection rates.

Operation Rhino. Inspector Crawford, Acting Chief Inspector Groves and Inspector
Hobson at Newcastle Railway Station, with everything including the kitchen sink!

Snowy weather conditions in the north of Scotland.

VICTIM SUPPORT

All police forces have victim support schemes, but the British Transport Police lead the field when it comes to speed of referrals. Initiatives developed during the 1990s, financed by a Home Office grant as well as money from the railway industry, have provided every station with a computer link to a terminal at Victim Support Headquarters in London. Here, details of all victims of personal crimes, e.g. rape, assault, etc., are recorded and the information sent by computer from local station to the Crime Desk; this, in turn, passes the information on to an appropriate group selected from a data base of over 450 groups. Preferably at the time the crime is reported, or as soon as is physically possible afterwards, every victim is given a leaflet detailing the purpose of victim support. Within 24 hours they can then be referred to a support group. In cases where immediate referral is required, officers can refer locally. To mark the BTP's and the railway industry's association with Victim Support, a locomotive was named *Victim Support* at a ceremony attended by the Princess Royal in 1994.

Assistant Chief Constable Alan Parker and the Princess Royal.

Among the fatalities dealt with by BTP officers on the railway lines are the inevitable suicides. In 1994/95 140 people chose to end their life in the path of a train. Officers are well trained to deal with these difficult situations. They are responsible for retrieving the body, identification, informing the next of kin and attending coroners inquests.

Many vagrants and sufferers of mental health problems frequent the Inner City stations, and to help understand and facilitate them, the Force is active in working with such mental health organisations as the National Schizophrenic Fellowship (NSF).

THE FUTURE AND PRIVATISATION

When the Government published plans to privatise the railways in 1992, concern and rumours immediately followed that the Force would be disbanded. The Railways Act of 1993, which provided for a restructured railway network, certainly created a need for a new constitution for the Force, and the Minister of Transport made repeated assurances that the policing of the railways would remain in the public domain. However, there was a danger of BTP having their jurisdiction removed during the passage of the Railways Bill, and as a result it was hastily re-drafted and enacted within weeks.

The Transport Police Jurisdiction Act of 1994 – only the second this century to pass through the Commons and the Lords in one day (the other being the Official Secrets Act of 1911) – maintains that the licensed operators of the railway services must contract BTP services, and allows for the appointment of 'Specials', unpaid and part-time, to support officers on their beat. In this way, the Force has been realigned to the railway industry, with whom it sets joint objectives.

PC Matt Payn

A range of vehicles are available to officers for police work.

The restructuring that began under Chief Constable O'Brien and Assistant Chief Constable Alan Parker, and which came into force in April 1992, has considerably heightened BTP focus and effectiveness. Decision-making now devolves from Force Headquarters to eight Areas within England, Scotland and Wales, allowing Force Headquarters to concentrate on setting values, maintaining standards, creating policy, auditing operations and providing essential expertise. Officers In Charge (OICs) have been appointed to every Police Station to manage the policing locally, thus increasing cost effectiveness and accountability at ground level.

October 1995. Traction Inspector Graham Petrie talking to Sergeant John Bullment (Exeter) after arriving at Plymouth with a 12-coach steam locomotive-hauled special passenger train. Both men travelled from Exeter to Plymouth and many hundreds of people turned out to watch the trains pass along the coast of South Devon.

POLICING INTO EUROPE

The Channel Tunnel represents a renaissance for the railway industry. By 1996 passengers will be able to step on a train in Manchester, for example, and three or four hours later step off in another country. To prepare for this major development, a Channel Tunnel project team, led by Chief Inspector Alistair McQueen, has been carrying out a tremendous amount of preparation – not only of operational procedures, but with the help of BTP Crime Prevention Officers, Ray Kelly and Barrie Wickens, advising owners of Channel Tunnel associated businesses on relevant aspects of crime prevention. In addition, a team of three Sergeants and 21 Constables have been trained for international operations by a package put together by Inspectors Todd and Cummings, HM Customs, the immigration authorities and the Corporation of London's Trading Standards Department (responsible for rabies control in London).

In 1993 Paul Traise-Roffe was appointed Force Liaison Officer, to build relationships between BTP and Forces throughout Europe. The following year saw officers officially begin their international duties. Reciprocal police, customs and immigration facilities are available at all destinations with access to the Police National Computer. Where differences in policing and legislation occur, compromises have to be agreed by all parties. For example, the Railway Byelaw concerning alcohol is unworkable through the Tunnel in its existing form, therefore a high police profile must be maintained whenever football fans are on board.

Kent Police have jurisdiction over Eurotunnel's Shuttle trains and police the Shuttle's terminal at Cheriton, near Folkestone.

The opening of the Channel Tunnel has brought opportunities and challenges to the whole nation that will change the way of policing in this country for ever. It is a challenge that BTP are facing head on. The Force's Mission Statement – 'Making our Railways the safest and enhancing the quality of life for customers and staff, whilst safeguarding the whole community' – speaks for itself, as do the Force values – 'Giving the best quality policing service which is caring, efficient, courteous and approachable in a way that is consultative, flexible and cost effective'.

BTP officers liaise with their counterparts at Paris Gare du Nord.

BRITISH TRANSPORT POLICE OFFICERS KILLED ON PEACETIME DUTY 1825 - 1995

29.09.1895	Detective Sergeant Robert Kidd, 37 yrs, LNWR at Wigan. Stabbed, during arrest.
10.08.1901	Detective Constable Thomas Hibb, 23 yrs, LNWR[1] at Birmingham. Beaten, found drowned.
05.12.1906	PC Ernest Moore, Midland Railway. Hit by Train, on patrol.
14.03.1907	PC George Leffe, 23 yrs, N.E. Railway. Stabbed, during disturbance.
19.08.1934	PC Alfred Haines, Brighton Railway[2]. Hit by train, crowd control.
25.01.1960	PC Walter Macmillan, 30 yrs, British Transport Police. Fall, chasing suspect.
23.11.1970	PC Keith Winter, 22 yrs, British Transport Police. Gas explosion.

---

[1] Possibly GWR

[2] Most likely a member of the Brighton Division of the Southern Railway Police. Until the 1st January 1923 it was the London, Brighton & South Coast Railway which ran to Brighton.

1820   Bow Street Runners working from magistrates courts in London

1825   Opening of the Stockton & Darlington Railway – Police Department in operation

1827   Liverpool & Manchester Railway employs police officers

1829   Metropolitan Police Act creates a formal force that is to be the model for city and county forces

1831   Special Constables Act enables Railway Companies to officially appoint Special Constables to preserve order on the construction sites, to patrol and protect the line and control movements of traffic

1835   Municipal Corporations Act grants counties the power to form their own forces

1838   Railways (Conveyance of Mails) Act requires railways to carry the mail as the Postmaster General dictates

1839   Royal Commission set up to decide the best means of establishing an efficient Constabulary

1840   Canal (Offences) Act enables navigation companies to appoint their own police officers

1842   The Metropolitan Police Force forms the first offical Detective Department
First Royal Train Journey

1856   County Police Act forces authorities to establish their own forces, with funding provided by the Government

1863 LNWR become the first Railway Police force to create its own Detective Department
First Underground Railway opened in London

1864 A German named Müller murders Thomas Briggs – the first murder to take place on the railways

1908 Police dogs first enter the Force at Hull Docks

1914 World War 1 begins

1919 First meeting of the Railway Police Federation

1921 Railways Act groups railway companies into 4 main groups: GWR, LNWR, SR & LMSR

1926 National Strike

1933 London Passenger Transport Board created by an Act of Parliament

1939 World War II declared

1946 Railway Police Training School purchased at Tadworth

1947 Transport Act nationalises the railways and their undertakings, such as ports, hotels, London Transport, inland waterways and long distance road haulage

1948 Brtitsh Transport Commission created

1956 Pay parity awarded by Lloyd Williams. Maxwell Johnson enquiry follows

1958 London Transport Police amalgamated into the British Transport Commission Police
Cadet training introduced

1959 First national Headquaters opens at Park Royal, London

1960 Warden Security Corps created

1961 Newsam Report published

1962 British Transport Commission Act passed
Transport Act abolishes British Transport Commission
Terry Shelton takes over the dog training school

1963 British Transport Commission Police changes name to British Transport Police
First Force Police Dog Trials held
Arthur West retires as Chief Constable, replaced by William O Gay
Great Train Robbery occurs

1964 British Transport Police Force Scheme laid before Parliament

1968 Tadworth closes and training continues at Home Office Schools and at the Railway Committee's school, New Lodge, Windsor

1971 Tadworth reopens

1972 Mr S Lawrence QPM investigates and reports on the Force

1973 Increase in football violence requires all fan-carrying trains to be routinely policed

1975 Mr Eric Haslam takes over as Chief Constable
Moorgate disaster

1978 Edmund Davies Report on the pay and conditions of police forces increases pay for Home Office Forces but not BTP

1979 Police Information System (PINS) introduced

1981   Mr Kenneth Ogram becomes Chief Constable
       Force Headquarters moves to Tavistock Place, London
       Specialist Search Dogs introduced to the Force

1984   New Dog School opens at Tadworth
       Miners Strike
       Police & Criminal Evidence Act passed

1985   Associated British Ports cease docks police contract
       Prosecution of Offenders Act passed
       Heysel Stadium disaster

1986   The ferry Koningen Beatrix returns to Parkeston Quay after
       rioting by football fans

1987   Kings Cross Fire

1988   Clapham Rail Crash

1989   Desmond O Brien suceeds Kenneth Ogram as Chief Constable
       Purley Rail Crash
       PanAm 747 explodes over Lockerbie
       Sealink cease ports police contract
       National Football Intelligence Unit formed

1991   Intense IRA bombing campaign against the railways begins

1992   Government publish plans to privatise the railways

1993   Railways Act provides for a restructured railway network

1994   IRA ceasefire
       Transport Police Jurisdiction Act passed, securing the future of
       the Force

1995   Channel Tunnel opens, providing high speed rail link to the
       Continent

Bibliography

A List of Non Home Office Forces of the British Isles, Reginald Hale

Alfred G, Peedle, *The Story of London Transport Police; Some Personal Recollections*, Friends of the London Transport Museum Newsletter

Appleby, Pauline, *How To Work With Dogs,* How To Books Ltd

Author unknown, *100 Years of the Central*

Author unknown, *A Short History of Policing London's Transport*

Barker, Theo, *Moving Millions – A Pictoral History of London Transport,* London Transport Museum

British Transport Police – A Short History, BTP Recruiting Dept

British Transport Police Annual Report 1994-95

British Transport Police – Official Reports:
Striking Miners
Purley Rail Crash
Clapham Rail Crash
Clapham
Koningen Beatrix
European Cup Final

British Transport Police Journals/Blue Line from 1958 to present day

Coogan, Tim Pat, *The IRA,* Harper Collins

Executive Summary – Desmond Fennell Enquiry

Gero, David, *Aviation Disasters*, Patrick Stephens Ltd

Gordon, Kevin, *The British Transport Police – A Brief History of the Training Centre,* Tadworth

Gordon, Kevin, *The British Transport Police – A History of Policing the Railways*

Graves, Charles, *London Transport At War,* Allmark Publishing

Groves, Keith, *The Miners Strike & The British Transport Police*

GWR Annual Report 1923 & 1931

Hadfield, Charles, *The Canal Age,* David & Charles

Hall, Stanley, *Railway Detectives – 150 Years of the Railway Inspectorate,* Ian Allan

Herbert, Barry, *All Stations to Murder – True Tales of Crime on the Railway,* Silver Link Publishing Ltd

Holloway, Sally, *Moorgate: Anatomy of a Railway Disaster,* David & Charles

Howson, HF, *London's Underground,* Ian Allan Ltd

Mike, Clarke, *The Leeds & Liverpool Canal,* Carnegie Press

Minutes of Meetings – Directors of the Banff Portsoy & Strathisla Railway Co 12.1.1859

Morgan, Kenneth O (Ed), *The Oxford Illustrated History of Britain,* Guild Publishing

O Gay, William, MA, *The Constable on the Track – An Account of Early Railway Police*

Otter, Randolph & Michael, Burnham, *British Transport Police 1947 to 1987 – An Historical Review*, BTP

Police Minute Book: Conference of Chiefs of Police 1942 – 1947

Public Records Office References:
Rail 667/485
Rail 312/130
Rail 667/487
Rail 667/633
Rail 312/130
Rail 632/541
AN/2/304
AN/3/34

Robottom, John, *A Social & Economic History of Industrial Britain*, Longman

The 95 Safety Drive: An Outline, BTP

The History, Powers & Duties of the British Transport Commission Police, Office of the Chief of Police, York

Thomas, Colin, Journal of the Police History Society No 9 1994, *The Origins of the British Transport Police*

Thomas, John & Turnock, David, *A Regional History of the Railways of Great Britain Vol 15, North of Scotland*, David St John Thomas

Vaughan, Adrian, *Grime & Glory – Tales of the Great Western 1892 – 1947*, John Murray (Publishers) Ltd

Whitbread, JR, *The Railway Policeman*, George G Harrap & Co

Useful Addresses

British Transport Police Historical Society
C/O Sgt Philip Trendall
Police Station
Stratford Railway Station
Great Eastern Road
London
E15 1AZ

Police History Society
C/O Martin Stallion ALA
28 Cornec Chase
Leigh on Sea
Essex SS9 5EW

Police Insignia Society
C/O Steve Daly
43 Hunters Way
Saffron Walden
Essex